AWAKEN
THE HEALER
WITHIN

AWAKEN THE HEALER WITHIN

A GUIDE TO TOTAL MIND & BODY HEALING

MARK EARLIX

MEDIA

Published 2023 by Gildan Media LLC
aka G&D Media
www.GandDmedia.com

First Edition: 2023

Front cover design by David Rheinhardt of Pyrographx

Interior design by Meghan Day Healey of Story Horse, LLC.

Library of Congress Cataloging-in-Publication Data is available upon request

ISBN: 978-1-7225-0655-1

10 9 8 7 6 5 4 3 2 1

This book is dedicated to God, for the years
of experience in understanding my gifts.

❧

To H.O.O.M., for showing me the easier way.

❧

To my friends, for being loving, supportive,
and full of insight.

❧

To all my students, apprentices, and drop-ins
for being my teachers of experience.

❧

For the many lifelong and newer friends that
I haven't yet met, who are seeking to understand
their relationship with their Self, their Source.

As I began to write,
A subtle, distant voice said,
"As you write, I'll be there.
Find me."

Contents

Introduction

In 1994, Penny, a psychotherapist, asked me to meet with her to discuss the possibility of my participating in one of her two-day seminars for the benefit of her clients. The purpose was to introduce my work to help them learn some simple dynamics about spiritual healing.

We arranged to meet at a local coffeehouse. As I sat waiting for her, I found myself thinking how wonderful this opportunity could be for me but how difficult it would be and how nervous I was about exposing my life's understandings to the world. I didn't think I was prepared. I wasn't sure what to say, nor did I ever dream or expect that what I was able to do in my life could be taught to others.

As soon as Penny sat down, we began to map out a plan. We decided to take turns speaking. She probed me with questions so I could prepare my portion of the presentation. I was not sure how I could possibly relate my experience with spiritual healing and make it available to each and every person.

My teachers warned me not to go public with what I am capable of doing "lest people come knocking at my door." They instructed that discretion and integrity were of the utmost importance. Discretion, they said, is important in order to let my light shine and let the truth be shown silently; that is the way of the Gnostic. But at this point, I have discerned from my heart those parts of my abilities that can be shared, including how they can be applied by anyone, as well as their source. Of course, there are certain aspects of my abilities that cannot be shared.

The following Saturday, I was introduced to Penny's twenty-five attendees. They were a diverse group from varied walks of life. I felt afraid that what I knew could not be taught. How could I convey what I felt inside and how I approached a particular healing experience? How could I teach what I envisioned? How could they accept what could possibly be happening within the person I work on or what that person might be seeing? I was anxious and frightened as I approached the podium.

Now it was my turn. As I started to talk, I found myself transformed. The words seemed as though they were coming from the ether around me and at the same time from the depths within me. I watched myself converting from introvert to extravert. I found myself in a mode of trust. The words and gestures flowed easily from my mouth, from within me, and I was excited.

I remember wondering what I would do if someone were to challenge me. Should I respectfully defend myself or gracefully sit down without further comment? But no one challenged me. They listened intently as the words flowed easily and flawlessly. They became captivated, like children listening to a story. They realized that I was credible, that what I was expressing was true for each person's life. I watched them listen with their mouths slightly open and wide-eyed. For the first time, I saw myself in this extraverted frame of expression. I enjoyed the feeling!

On this particular Saturday, I spoke for a short while, and then it was Penny's turn. When it was my turn to speak again, I felt good enough to take the people through an exercise. It was a closed-eyes exercise my teachers had given me twenty-five years earlier. Its purpose was to help them to "see" in a more focused way into the nonlinear world.

Halfway through the exercise, a young woman, Melinda, decided to peek, so she opened her eyes and intently watched as I continued. Melinda was able to naturally focus on nonlinear perceptions: she was sometimes able to see things that weren't normally captured by others. Something had changed in her; the exercise was helping to open something more within her. Then the greatest of all my fears came to face me.

First, some background information. Twenty-three years prior to this first seminar, I was living in Fort Worth, Texas. One evening, I had gone to a bar filled with hundreds of people. While sitting at a small table in the front near the door, a large, rugged-faced man in a leather jacket approached me. He looked at me and simply asked, "Who are you really?" I told him my name was Mark Earlix, and that I loved God. He began asking me questions about God. I found that the answers came easily. He continued with his questions, and the words came pouring out of my mouth.

As I looked up, I saw that others were starting to gather around the table. Several others had also started to ask questions; my answers also came easily. For some unknown reasons, chatter about me began to spread throughout the bar. Others suffering with health problems and injuries approached and asked for healing. I complied and began to work on many people there while still in my seat, hands outstretched.

This went on for quite a while (I'd lost track of the time) when a young man edged himself toward the side of the table and urgently asked me to follow him toward the back of the bar where someone needed help. Without thinking, I quickly got up and followed him to a table further into the bar, where four people were seated. They found a chair for me and asked me to sit with them. The fellow across from me rolled up his right sleeve to show me a raised, deep red, irritated rash that ran the length of his arm. He grimaced and said, "It itches and hurts like hell." He asked if I could help him.

I looked deeply into his eyes and nodded. Without words, I reached over the table and placed both my hands on the darkest red area. I prayed within myself for a couple of moments. As I opened my eyes, I saw that many others were gathering and waiting to see what was going on and what was going to come from my actions. I then put my arms back to my side. The fellow rubbed his arm several times and then began to smile at me as the redness and hurt dissipated.

The young woman sitting next to him watched his reaction, looked at his arm, then at me, back again at him, and she immediately became hysterical. Tears streamed from

her eyes and her face was dark red. She began scream-
ing incoherently and uncontrollably as she kept thrusting
her hands with outstretched fingers pointing at me. I froze
inside; I did not know what to do. The people at and around
the table watched speechlessly. The screams prompted
hundreds of silent eyes from all around to look at me. I
wanted to slump down in fear as numbness and a flush
overtook me.

Instead, I found the strength within myself to remain
upright. I wanted desperately to get out of there. As I began
to garner the strength to stand to leave, something was
beginning to happen inside me. An unknown, unexperi-
enced power and force came over me. I shot up on my feet,
reached across the table with my right hand, and waved
the outstretched hand quickly over the man's arm, knowing that the healing would be taken away as easily as it had
been given.

Hurriedly, I began to leave, feeling as if I had done something horrible and unfathomably unconscionable. As I
pushed and wove my way through the crowd of watching,
confused, and wondering eyes, I glanced back and saw the
fellow holding his arm as the pain and redness returned.
At the same moment, the young woman stopped crying. I
thought I heard her thinking, or saying, "This is the way it's
supposed to be." I never went back.

Fast forward to the Saturday seminar. Here I was, participating in this seminar and facing a similar dilemma. The
woman who peeked was crying hysterically as she pointed
toward me. Again, I found myself becoming speechless
and numb. But this time I forced myself to stay and began
to make excuses for what had happened. I did not want to

participate in this seminar anymore, and I clamped down in fear, feeling that this wasn't something that people were ready to accept. This was my excuse in my younger years. This dilemma and avoidance were the very dynamic that I was about to work out in life.

I have since learned that these experiences were there for me as stepping stones in my learning process. I was immature, inexperienced. I encountered these situations to break the mold of introducing my teachings. They were for me to take and grow with in a new, different, and meaningful way, so that I could understand how to live outside of my enclosed world and go forth into the world I was born to serve. These experiences, which later developed into wisdom, were also there so that I could help others realize that they too can be free.

It is important for me to help people understand that everything is really OK, that we are not unloved or uncared for. We are not alone; we can find reprieve from the chaos and fear in our lives. It really is OK to rediscover the trust that we lost at such an early age.

God, the Creator, the Divinity Within, is alive and well within us. God, in his, her, or its way, is telling us that we have an ability to find its unique and individualized expression within. We also learn that none of this is possible without trust. This is when the miracles flow—although not supernaturally, because we find that miracles are really the way things naturally happen within the activity of life. Great things can happen with us too, as we realize the possibilities of natural, nonlinear life.

Each and every one of us has the ability to amend our life's dramas and traumas. We can dissipate disease and infirmities, and we can ease discomfort so that some or all of the effects are gone. The tissue will no longer be inflamed, the bones become straightened, and stresses can melt. The body heats up, or we feel the electrical charge or air flowing through us; then we feel clear inside. It is as though we flicked on a switch in a darkened room, and the shadows are no longer there. This could happen in the twinkling of an eye, and even faster. It is a way of healing.

All of this, and much more, will be related to you in this book. You will realize that you too have the ability to work with healing, not only for yourself but for others. This is a book for self-help and healing. It is also an extensive training program for how to heal and be healed physically, emotionally, and mentally. This book can help you to actualize understandings and realities that you have only dreamt of, that you thought only a select few could attain. You can feel better not only in your body but about yourself.

This book is about the ability to recreate in the Divine image. We are here to strive for perfection. Our purpose is to find the ability to love ourselves so that Self can express its unconditional love. This will become clearer as you read on and delve more into this unlimited, nonlinear world, which is much greater than our imaginations can conjure up.

It is written that we are created in the image of God. If that is true, we also have the ability to recreate in that image. And if that is true, then we are cocreators.

Preparation

Judgment of what we witness,
In ourselves, others and situations,
Is the flow of destruction
And is a learned pattern of memories,
Not a Being way.

This book will show you how to heal. You will realize that you too have the ability to heal, not only yourself, but others as well. You will learn to create what you have only dreamt of and accomplish what you thought that only a select few could attain. You will discover that you can feel better not only physically, but also emotionally and mentally.

This book is about the ability to replicate and recreate in the Divine image. After all, we are here in this life to strive for perfection. You will be invited to delve into the unlimited, nonlinear world that we live with and lives within us. The world of what we call the Nameless One, the Universal Mind, Creator, Self, or God, which is much greater than our imaginations can possibly conceive. I can help you to pursue your purpose in life—to love yourself, to recognize the ideal perfection in yourself so that the Divine Self living within you can express itself through you. It is the Great Mind of Godliness that patiently awaits its rediscovery.

This is the information we already carry within us; we already have experience of its wisdom. We need only to remember this truth from within us.

I can share with you some ideas and understandings from my experience. I will offer you many exercises that, if practiced, will bring quick results and a greater understanding from your own Self. The teachings I present are a compilation of teachings, experiences, and revelations that I have received from within myself and from my work as a healer and intuitive. This wisdom will be my gift to you in this book.

The Time Is Now

You have probably opened this book because you know it's your time to go through another change, whether gentle or dramatic. All of our experiences have enabled us to grow to a greater maturity so that we can understand and deepen aspects of our lives that we may have strived to make sense of since childhood.

Perhaps you have always felt there is more to you than what others see in you. Perhaps you feel there is more to this world than you have been taught to believe. Perhaps most of your life you have always felt uncomfortable, some-how different, but without knowing why or where to go with this deeply rooted feeling. Or maybe you feel that there is a simple and direct calling in your life. In all of life's lessons, you might have sensed something didn't feel true to you or was being left out. Perhaps you are looking for your life's purpose and feel you won't be fulfilled without it. Perhaps you are yearning to fill the gap between the possibilities and realities of your life. You're ready for a change.

Most people facing life's changing experiences go through this discomfort, even they have longed for it in order to find more meaning in their existence. Change may be especially scary if, for your own sense of safety, you've had to cover up or change your deepest thoughts and feelings or had to fight for everything you have.

My intention in this book is to help you answer many of the questions you have had all your life—things of which you have had glimpses but have been unable to completely process thus far. The change you gain from this text will come from within you.

My purpose is to empower you to recognize your greatness and to support you in striving for your personal perfection and wholeness. As you internally respond to what you read and you practice the exercises I suggest, you may experience either subtle or dramatic shifts in your perception of what is real. I call this process of internalizing these experiences "alchemical." Your life will change.

Metamorphosis

Many people are living lives that lack any expression of conscious self-love. They may have experienced an absence of encouraging love in their developmental years, which has resulted in their inability to love and to be loved as the years go on.

Some of us were raised in that kind of experience. We learned to make excuses for ourselves in thought, conversation, and action. We deftly protected ourselves. We taught ourselves (and learned this lesson all too well) to divert ourselves from feeling the discomforts of growth. Instead, we have gotten ourselves into a state of false comfort. We don't realize we have the ability to create real comfort for ourselves and reignite the love that has eluded us.

We often experience a sense of lack in life—not only lack of love and lack of friendship, but of a good job, income, self-worth . . . you name it. That very sense of lack is a call to recognize Self, the Divinity Within and allow it to teach us what we have dismissed. We must experience and face our shortfalls and downfalls in order to work them out. We do this by identifying where they came from—what I call their *causal moment*—so we can amend our lives. Working them out may be less difficult than you imagine.

These very shortcomings are in reality stepping stones with which we have come into birth. That is why they are there in the first place. Once we finally work these things out in ourselves, we can finally go on to our other work in the evolutionary process.

All these experiences are actually here to help us become aware of our abilities and tools. Once we learn how to respond to problematic situations with our internal resources, we'll observe these experiences of lack as things we've created ourselves. We can finally say to them, "Oh, I see you; you're trying to become part of me, so I can act you out in my life in the same way I've always done. Well, I now choose otherwise, so stand back and wait here; I will be right back."

This sense of lack offers an opportunity for us to recognize that it is actually external to our psyche. We can choose to consciously review and adjust our usual reactions. All that is required is that we identify our problematic situations as "conversations" that started at some time from certain dramas and traumas. We can then understand that we don't have to continually relive these old conversations. As we internalize this realization and put it in action, the old patterns no longer affect us as dramatically; nor are we participating in them or reacting to them as often.

As you read this book, you will be delving into the non-physical, nonlinear part of the universe, where there is no separation between time, place, or space. You have been moving toward this experience all your life. Now is your time to actually experience Universal Self, God, Divinity Within.

There are many names and phrases to represent this Nameless One: God, Krishna, Self, Universe, Yahweh, Buddha, Christ, Jesus, and many others. I mostly refer to the Universal Self. These name all represent the same living consciousness that underlies and connects everything. We are created in the image of this Nameless One, this Universal Self, so it is not different from us. We all have this Self within. It carries the consciousness of power, force, and energy to manifest our thoughts in the immediate and externalized world around us through the linear and nonlinear world within us. It also enables us to change our thoughts and beliefs at any moment . . . in constant conscious creation. This is the gift of free will that has been shared with us.

In reality, there is no such thing as free will. There is no fate or destiny . . . except for one.

As for reincarnation and coming back again and again, why? The only reason to reincarnate would be to get to know ourselves. This is the only reason for fate and destiny. The innate ability of free will is to get to know ourselves. The Universal Mind, Creator, God, is constantly and gently guiding us back into getting us to know our Self.

This book will provide exercises and explanations to help you to live in the experience of the Self, with all its powerful dynamics and gifts. It will help you to realize the healing of yourself and others. What a statement! Could it be true?

The Beginning

I returned home from Vietnam in 1970. I was deeply wounded, emotionally and spiritually. I carried an anxiety that would not let me be still or at peace inside. I felt unsettled in everything and with everyone I met. I also felt that every goal I had was unsatisfying. I had to keep moving. I quit jobs or was fired. I was depressed and losing my desire for food, so my body became more and more malnourished. My emotional and mental capacities weren't functioning properly. I was down and out—truly in dire straits.

I drifted, traveling around the country, taking jobs that I couldn't hold longer than a week, sometimes not even for a day. My parents had just about given up on me; they didn't know what to do or say to help me. In those days there was no term for posttraumatic stress disorder (PTSD), much less any therapy to alleviate the emotional pain. Veterans coming back from Vietnam just got a few days of R and

R in Japan or some other pleasant place before being sent home—if they were lucky. I wasn't.

Over the next two years, I was usually drunk or and emotionally or physically violent with myself or with others. I didn't care if I got hurt or hurt others. I couldn't stay in a relationship for more than a few days. For a short while, I was homeless, living on the streets of Chicago. Finally, I wound up in Arizona, at the end of my rope, always hoping for a reprieve in life. I carried an anxiety that wouldn't let me be still inside. I felt unsettled in everything and with every person I met. I also felt that I had to keep moving. I lost my joy to depression. I decided to end my life.

On the day I decided to commit suicide, I looked around as though I was saying goodbye and focused on a pile of clothes lying on the floor of the little bungalow I lived in. The only thing that I could focus on was my dirty laundry. This one, simple, unimportant thing in life caught my attention. I knew that my parents would have to come here to get my body. They would come in and see me lying amidst my dirty laundry. How embarrassing! I thought. That would make it even worse for them. I decided I would first go to the laundromat and wash my clothes; then I would come back and kill myself.

With tunnel vision, I focused on my dirty laundry, quickly and intently jamming it into my duffel bag, one piece at a time. I left the little bungalow and began walking to the laundromat two blocks away. As I got to the sidewalk, somewhere in the back of my mind I heard a car horn honking incessantly. At first it seemed far away, but as I switched my focus, I realized the car was right next to me. It was breaking into my tunnel vision and my quest to do my laundry. I was angry. I didn't want my focus to be changed.

I turned around and saw two women in the car. I yelled at them to leave me alone. The honking continued. The women yelled to me, "We'll give you a ride!" I ignored them and kept on walking. They persisted, and after a few minutes I dropped my resistance. I decided that it would be of no consequence to me if I got into their car. Finally, after looking at their faces to see if I could detect some motivation for giving me a ride, I got into the car and told them to take me to the laundromat.

The women introduced themselves as Patricia and Diane. As Patricia drove, she began telling me my life history. Patricia told me things she could never have known. I had no idea how she knew these things, and my focus went back to the dirty laundry. As we drove past the launderette, I yelled, "Hey! Let me out!"

"No," Patricia answered. "We're going to get something to eat, and we want you to come with us," and kept on driving. As she drove, Patricia continued to relate several details of my life with accuracy, while Diane sat there, smiling or slightly chuckling most of the time. As Patricia spoke, she was unemotional, almost indifferent, but she conveyed a feeling of wanting to tell me the truth of what they somehow knew and continued to describe in detail.

"Who are you? How do you know these things about me?" I was amazed and confused.

We pulled into a Mexican restaurant. At that time, I hated Mexican food, but they insisted I come inside and get something to eat. "The food is great," they promised.

Finally I followed them in and had the best chimichangas I'd ever eaten in my life.

During the meal, Patricia and Diane told me more truths about my life. I couldn't explain how they could possibly know all the details. After we ate, they gladly drove me to the laundromat, and as they were dropping me off, I asked them how I could find them again. I *needed* to find them again.

As they started to drive away, Diane quickly shouted out their address and said goodbye. I didn't have a chance to write it down before they drove away, and I yelled after them, "Wait! I have no memory! I can't remember that!" But they were gone, and so was the address, lost in the recesses of my troubled mind. I didn't know how I would ever find them again.

Somehow, from the depths of my memory, her voice with the address remained in my head. I had remembered and known how to find them. At seven that same night, I was knocking on their door. They opened the door, smiled, welcomed me in, and offered a home-cooked meal. A few days after that, I moved in with them. They gave me a place to live and found me a job. This was the first job I was able to keep for more than several days. It lasted six months.

I'd found two people (or should I say that they found me) who let me express the real me inside. They listened to me daily, and I listened to little pieces of their life stories, though they never told me much about who they were. We played, worked, and ate meals together. They were always happy inside, and their joy influenced my life enough that I wanted to be that way too. I found myself slowly changing to something I'd longed for inside—to something that was hidden so deeply and from so long ago within me. This was one of the happiest times than I had been in years, at least since before I'd gone to Nam.

One day they informed me they were moving to San Francisco, and Patricia went her way with intentions of joining us later as Diane and I left together. I had found two people who helped me to express a more real me and a joy inside of me. I was not about to leave them.

Soon after Diane and I arrived in San Francisco, we went to a three-story Gothic-style building. As I walked in, there was a crowd of regular-looking people milling about in the waiting area. Diane then told me that I was going to stand before the Esoteric Council, and all that I could conjure up in my mind was, "Oh, OK." I sat down and waited for my turn to be interviewed by the council that Diane had just told me about. I watched the secretary receive calls and tell others it was their turn to go upstairs.

When it was my turn, the secretary walked me up the stairs and opened a door that led into a very large room. The room was filled with people, older, younger, men, women ... all completely silent. There was a total stillness in the room, and everyone was watching me. Then I noticed a balding older gentleman with white hair, puffing on a pipe. He smiled at me and ended the silence by saying, "Welcome! I'm Paul. Have a seat."

I sat next to him at his desk. The other people continued to watch me in silence. Paul asked, "What's your name? What religion are you?" I told him my name and said that I was Jewish.

"Oh!" he said, "We have a lot of Jewish people here. You'll enjoy it. Welcome!"

I didn't know I had made a commitment to be there yet. At that time, I thought I would probably continue to travel all over the country. I didn't know what was going on or whether they were going to do something weird to me— maybe try to indoctrinate me into some kind of a cult.

Paul asked, "Well, Mark, what are you doing here?" I thought for a moment and answered, "I don't know." As I said this, I found myself delving deep into many layers of thought through what seemed to be fifteen or twenty secret, barren rooms within myself. As I shot through each of these empty cells within the recesses of my mind, I heard myself at a distance repeating over and over again, "I don't know, I don't know." Finally, Paul said with a smile, "OK, we believe you." It was as though I snapped out of it! At the end of our meeting, Paul introduced me to a fellow named John, who was designated as my novice master and teacher.

When the interview was all over (which turned out to be for less than ten minutes), they accepted me and took me in, although they never actually said, "We accept you." They would give me a place to sleep, food to eat, and a place to work. No requirements were made of me. I didn't have to turn over my worldly goods (not that I had many).

From that day forward, my entire life changed. I felt and knew I was in a special place. While there, I began to discover hidden aspects of my life and begin my journey to learn what might be real for me. It was the early 1970s, an era of mystique, enchantment, and extraordinary experiences for many people like me.

The first day, John instructed me to go across the street to a little chapel and kneel before the Mary shrine there. No one told me what a Mary shrine was, why I should kneel, or what I should do once I did kneel. I was told that someone would pick me up in about thirty minutes to show me where I was going to stay and get me something to eat. After saying goodbye to the small man, who looked like Mr. Magoo, I walked downstairs, crossed the street, and knocked on the chapel door. A man in a brown robe opened the door and asked if he could help me. I told him I was sent to the chapel from across the street.

"Fine," he said. "But you don't have to knock. This is a chapel." I walked in. There was no one in this dim, candlelit room. As he started to leave, I stopped him. "Where is the Mary shrine?"

"Over there," he quizzically pointed. "Anything else?"

"Yeah," I said. "How do you kneel?"

He looked at me strangely. "Are you serious?"

"Yeah," I replied.

He briskly walked me over to the shrine and hesitantly showed me how to kneel. "How come you don't know this?"

"I'm Jewish," I answered.

"Oh, we have lots of people here who are Jewish," he said and left without saying goodbye.

The door made a creaking sound as it closed behind him. If anyone else opened the door, it would creak again, so I figured that this was the perfect opportunity to take a nap: if the door opened, I would wake up, and it would look as if I were still awake when someone arrived to get me. Against the wall was a little table with a red rose in a beautiful lead crystal vase with a beautiful handmade lace doily under it.

On the wall above the table hung a slightly tilted picture of a woman with a beautiful face and a white veil covering her head. I straightened out the picture and then tilted it several times, because it looked as if the woman in the picture were looking at me. Then I moved the table around so it was more to my liking and comfort. Out of boredom, I began picking the petals off the rose and put them in my pocket to hide the evidence of what I'd done.

I became very tired and gently laid my head down on the table to rest. As my head went down with my eyes shut, I found myself semiconsciously drifting into an altogether different place.

This dreamlike place reminded me of the old English countryside, with hedges cut into a large maze that went on forever in all directions. I stood there for a moment. Suddenly, somewhere in the maze, there was a vision of myself standing near a light-brown earthen road, about twenty feet wide. I stood in a low-cut grassy area, next to an old-fashioned wrought-iron park bench. The bench was quite ornate, with thin wood slats.

To my left, the road led into a lush, dark green forest. There was an archway where the road led into the forest, but I couldn't see anything as I tried looking into the darkness inside. To my right, the road led to what looked like an ancient stone monastery with a drawbridge like those you see on old castles with moats (though there was no water). The door, attached by two huge chains, lowered and became a ramp as it opened. The chains made a distinctly clear sound without reverberation as the door lowered.

From out of this stone structure came a procession of monks. There were ten rows of them, four across, wearing long, brown, hooded robes that completely covered their heads, hands, and feet. Where their faces should have been,

I saw what I could only describe as an opalescent blackness. It was almost like looking into a shiny piece of coal with an endless depth. The monks walked by without acknowledging me, except for one. He stepped out from his place in the third column of the last row. He took his arms out from his sleeves and pushed his hood back, and I saw he had a beautiful face, very masculine but at the same time fragile and ethereal. He had shiny black hair. I was struck by how magnificent he looked.

He came over to me and introduced himself as Raphael. As soon as he'd introduced himself, I noticed that we were sitting, and Raphael began lecturing and informing me about the understandings of healing. The more he talked, the more I questioned, and the more he explained, the more questions he brought up for me.

To this day, I still don't remember all of his words; I only know that everything he said was instilled within me forever. I asked him many, many questions. As he answered every one, the answers resonated within me, and I knew and accepted what he said was true. Our conversation centered completely on healing and its meanings.

Only later would I understand that all my life, with all of its experiences, had led me to this moment. Since the day I was born, my path had been set, totally unbeknownst to me, and now the spiritual side was about to take form. I'd been waiting for this moment throughout the joyful experiences of my life as well as the dramatic and traumatic ones. In this moment, in this vision, I changed in a way that later manifested in the mental and physical world around me.

The procession of monks then returned, walking the brown earthen road back toward the monastery. Raphael stood and put his hood back on, tucked his arms into his sleeves, and resumed his place in the line. I noticed that he didn't say goodbye to me, knowing that it wasn't necessary. The monks reentered the stone building, and the ramp door went back up.

At that moment, I felt someone tap me on the shoulder. I swung my head around. I found myself back in the little chapel. The fellow tapping me on the shoulder began to speak meekly: "I'm sorry I'm late, but I'm here to get you something to eat and show you where you will be sleeping."

"OK," I replied, and we left the chapel. Once the door of the chapel opened to the outside, I noticed that the daylight was gone. I looked at my watch. I had been in the chapel for five and a half hours! At that moment, I regarded what happened in the chapel as the greatest dream I had ever experienced in my life. I felt fantastic.

The Change

As we walked away from the little basement chapel, I knew that something had changed in me. I was unsure what the difference was, but the thought crossed my mind that I felt satisfaction—as though I had found something out about myself that had never occurred to me before, something unique and important. Then I said to myself that it had just been a wonderful dream, although it helped me feel rested, relaxed, relieved, and satisfied inside. But the memory of the dream kept returning over the next several days and seemed as real in memory as it had felt in the chapel.

The next morning, I was outside the house on San Francisco's Steiner Street, where I was staying, waiting for a ride to the new job that had been arranged for me. I would be working at a bookstore called the Rainbow Bridge, building bookshelves. I had absolutely no knowledge of how to do this, but it was to be my job for the next several days while I was with this new and strange group of people.

At 7:00 a.m., very little traffic moved along Steiner Street. A block away, I noticed a street bum purposefully making his way toward me. I watched him approach with an increasing sense of dread. I thought, "This guy is going to spit on me, shoot me, knife me, or try to do something else really vile to me." I stood in a defensive position, ready for whatever he was going to do. He was a short man, with greasy hair, tattered clothing, and a very unkempt appearance. He approached until he stood directly in front of me, and said, "Put your hands on my head."

"What?" I said, mystified.

"Put your hands on my head," he repeated, staring directly into my eyes.

Strangely, I had relaxed and no longer felt this man was a threat. No one was nearby watching to embarrass me, so I put my hands on his head. I felt dirt and grease, and then I felt a curious sensation coming from my hands, or from him, or from both of us. Whatever it was, I'd never felt anything like it before. The sensation lasted for five to seven seconds and then went away. Then the bum said, "Take your hands down."

I took my hands down from his head, totally speechless. For several seconds, he continued to stare into my eyes without emotion and finally said, "Thanks for taking my headache away." He walked away, and I never saw him again.

My ride arrived, and I went to the bookstore and started my training in building bookshelves. At lunchtime, a fellow named Richard, who also worked there, came up to me, and said, "I've got a horrible headache."

I didn't know why he would tell me this, and I said, "So?"

He looked right down at me and repeated, "I've got a headache."

I suddenly remembered my dream in the chapel the night before, my discussion about healing with the monk Raphael, and of course my experience that morning with the street bum. So I said, "Can I try something really strange with you?"

"Sure," he replied. I reached up and put my hands on his head. I felt the same sensation as I had before, but this time it only lasted a couple of seconds. The feeling dissipated, and I took my hands down.

Richard looked at me in a funny way and said, "How in the hell did you do that?"

"I don't know," I said. Much later, I asked Richard why he had initially approached me. His only answer was that he'd just felt compelled to tell me about his headache.

These strange occurrences were soon to become routine events in my life. Later I realized that the night before and this day marked an initiation into the work I was to grow into for the rest of my life.

Ever since that day in 1970, I have been working to develop this ability within me. Beginning then, I began practicing my techniques. I would work to heal people every chance I got. I knew that it was a strange gift that back then I couldn't go public with. For the next fifteen years, I focused exclusively on those most in need, like street people—the homeless, gang members, addicts, and alcoholics—anyone I thought I could help but who would not want or be able to find me later.

Three months after I joined the Order, I was directed to Fort Worth, Texas. Once there, I continued my silent, mostly unnoticed work with healing. I went into my healing mode every chance I could, with every stranger I met that was not well. Even if there wasn't anything wrong with them, I still threw my hands on top of their heads.

At one time, I had a job at a Bonanza restaurant. As the large staff of employees began to learn that I worked with healing, they would come around and watch me do this hands-on work, even during the busiest hours.

But there was a complication. From the first day I consciously started working on healing others, I began to take on their traumas and pains. Each day I would go home with a sore throat, pneumonia, or some other illness. I had sore muscles, headaches, migraines, sore throats, and awful lung inflammations. Once I even got someone else's black eye.

Every day, when I came home and walked through the front door, my teacher would ask, "What the hell happened to you?"

"I don't know," I'd answer, "but it was a lot of fun!" I'd tell him all my wondrous stories. And each day he would always say, "When are you going to learn, Mark; when are you going to learn?" I thought it was all so wonderful. He would put his hands on my head and get rid of my symptoms. I sometimes felt the strange sensations emanating from his hands into my head and then flowing to the parts of my body that had taken on sickness or injuries from others. He would send me to bed and have someone bring me a glass of grapefruit juice, which would be my dinner. The next morning, I would be almost fine and ready to go back to work.

But after a time, my body became weaker and so low on energy that my health started to break down and I would get a sick feeling for longer periods of time. My life force was becoming depleted from taking on others' symptoms and illnesses. One day on the bus on the way to work, I decided not to heal anyone ever again. I was tired of being sick, of being tired, of taking on all the aches and pains of those I healed. I decided I was going to quit this healing thing for-ever so that my own health might return.

I went to work that day feeling resolute in knowing I would never work with healing again, even though it was fun when I did. Up until that day, I had gone to work and put my hands on people for practice and attention, to prove to myself and others that I could heal. Now I was done with all of that forever.

Sitting on the bus on the way to work, I thought, "I'm never going to work with healing again." I told God, "Take this damned gift; I don't want it!" It felt good to have this resolved in my mind.

As soon as I got to work, an older woman, followed by an entourage of coworkers who wanted to watch me work on her, came up and said, "She has a massive migraine. Take it away from her." Other employees heard what was going to happen and began gathering around me. I was caught up in the thoughts and expectations of those gathered around: "Whoa, he's going to be healing her!"

It felt like a party. So I told the woman to sit down. I took off my coat and put my hands on her head. I felt bad for her that she was suffering. Then I remembered, "Oh my God! I'm going to get a migraine. I can't get this!"

At that moment a new thought came into my mind: if this healing thing began happening to me without my having any real knowledge of what was going on, then maybe it wasn't me doing this in the first place. I realized that if this was true, I could go back to how it was the first time, when I had put my hands on that bum's head in San Francisco. I didn't get a headache when I worked on him. I didn't even know what to expect, nor did I even have any idea what spirituality was.

I went ahead and put my hands on the woman's head, and at the same time, I said, "God, I don't want this migraine. You take it, God." My logic was that if God had the migraine, then I wouldn't get one. I began to chant in a cadence to myself inside, "You get this migraine, God, you get this migraine, God." I pictured God getting this woman's massive migraine.

I felt the familiar happen: a flow of energy traveling through me, which after a minute began to dissipate—an indicator that everything was done on my part. I put my hands down. The woman looked at me with an unsure gaze and said, "Thanks! It's gone. I don't feel it!" I was glad for her and then realized I didn't have a migraine either.

Since that day, I have not taken on others' illnesses, because I have realized it is not me doing the healing in the first place. All the symptoms I had felt for the previous three months were there for my growth, to prove to me the reality of my healing ability and to build compassion, confidence, and trust in something much greater than myself. I realized I no longer had to take on any illnesses, ailments, injuries, or anything else from another person.

Teaching Others to Heal

In 1994, even though more and more people were asking me to teach them how to heal, I still felt I couldn't go public with my abilities. Suddenly it seemed many people were asking me to teach them.

The workshop with Penny, which I mentioned in the introduction, brought out my ability to write the information down so that I could convey it to others. The first draft was difficult and a little rough around the edges. Initially we came up with enough for a half-day program of lectures and activities. I was sure that once the seminar started, people would want more information and understanding. Over the next couple of weeks, I revised and expanded the program into a full day's schedule. At that moment, I realized I could teach some aspects of what I do. And I have been teaching healing since then.

The esoteric order is no more. Since then, several branches, organizations, and affiliations have been formed by various members to carry on the teachings. Some have been directed into Eastern Orthodoxy, some into carrying on the initiatory process, and others into archiving the vast amounts of information in the Order. The former members of the Order have been integrated into various aspects of society and the world.

I have been ordained by my peers and by a greater lineage, first as a priest and in the latter years as a master teacher and healer. I am growing and will continue to expand my understanding for the rest of my life. I know that what I am doing now is only the beginning of what is still to come.

During one particular initiatory process in the Order back in 1973, I was guided through an experience of understanding my role in this world: there was a spiritual implosion of light, along with a physical change, within me. At this time, I first became conscious of this light, although I didn't know that it was to become my gift, my goal, and my tool. I also realize that it is much more than I am. Actually, there is no living person, plant, animal or element that doesn't have it. But with our complex consciousness, we have the opportunity to become more aware and more able to utilize this living light in life.

This light, a divine intelligence, is the source of our guidance and direction. The light has a consciousness, an intelligence. It knows what to do, either with or without our involvement. It uses us; we are its vehicles for reaching others, as well as our own selves, in order to be conscious and aware. I use this light to help others heal. More importantly, I have learned that anyone can use this light. I'm more fluent in utilizing it simply because I have practiced more. You can choose to practice too. If you do, you'll find that you can do what I can do with healing, and even more. It will happen naturally even without your belief that you will be able to heal others.

During the many years I've spent developing and experiencing these skills of healing, I've come to realize that anyone can do this. Through my teaching, I have learned that people have not only gained insight into the act of healing but have found other subtle changes in their lives as well. They felt better, more whole, and less troubled. They were growing on a spiritual level they hadn't anticipated. An unspoken void in their lives was being filled.

3

It's All Within:
Spiritual Discernment

Behold that which patiently waits within
And be whole.

I used to work at Motorola as a repair technician. I worked on circuit boards that had tiny chips about ⅛ inch long and ¹⁄₃₂ inch wide. These were receiver and transceiver mechanisms for electronic signals for cell phones and other products. If one of these circuit boards was even a little bit off, the whole mechanism would be off too. There would be no complete circuit and therefore no signal.

As people, we are very similar: within us, we carry representations like those of the little chips. Our nervous system carries electrical impulses and waves through us. These signals carry information through and around us, extending out into the universe. If a neurological response in our bodies is off, thoughts can be distorted, and our emotional, verbal, and physical actions will reflect that. At the same time, this distortion helps us recognize that something just isn't right.

As we learn about the intuitive perception process within us, we will find ourselves more in sync with the universe. This intuitive process helps to make us more conscious of our inner knowing and calls it into action. We hear and see through this knowing, which is within ourselves. The ancient mystics referred to it as the still, small voice within. As we recognize and acknowledge this, its voice grows louder and clearer, and it gets brighter in sight. *You will find that you will be able to see with your ears and hear with your eyes.* This is what I call *knowing.*

In hearing this still, small voice within, you will be better prepared to go forth and be a greater you. As you begin to heal yourself, you will find that the immediate world around you is also being healed.

Many people have traveled seeking enlightenment in far-flung spiritual centers such as those in the Himalayas. Once they have given up their money and belongings and spent time with great teachers, the teachers say, "Go home. It's all within you." And they are right! That's where it is. Everything is within us.

As we delve further into this study, we will tap into that still, small voice within, which has been waiting all our lives. It is in constant flow, always guiding and directing us. It will serve us in our physiological and emotional healing.

But how can we possibly heal anything or anyone that's already made perfect in the Creator's image? We are the ones who have abused and distorted the image. We are the cocreators and can be destroyed by the dramas and traumas we have created in our lives. It is the acceptance of these dramas and traumas that needs healing. These are the things we can work on now.

While working with this book, you may experience emotional catharsis or life changes as well as physiological, biological, and emotional healing. You may notice yourself going through changes immediately, when you complete the exercises presented here, or for the rest of your life. If you apply this book to your life, you will experience healing. You will learn a variety of healing techniques and spiritual exercises that will help you to go through life more simply and easily. You can begin to live without the daily conversations that have embroiled you in dramas and traumas. You will change your perception of what life is. If you choose, you can also help others in ways you haven't dreamt of before.

As you go through these dynamic processes, you will become more objective about your life, more able to recognize the entrapment of your own dramas and to be less affected by them. You will feel more centered and physically and emotionally free.

You will also be able to observe other people as they act in ways that are out of integrity and to understand what they are actually acting out, and why. From this perspective, you will be less likely to stand in judgment of them, because you will realize they are acting in the way they were taught and are doing the best they know, regardless of whether these are constructive or destructive behaviors.

In the following chapters, I will introduce a variety of philosophical concepts, definitions, ideas, and experiential work that will lay the foundation for your understanding of healing. These are not tied to any religion or connected with any church. I ask you to detach yourself from any of the current religious meanings of these terms while reading this book, and concentrate on understanding the philosophical concepts I present. I request you to have a big-picture concept that will help you rethink your understandings in life.

4

Spiritual Philosophy

Self sees you without judgment.
Self sees the truth,
But you are never condemned.
God does not reprimand
Or make guilty.

I. Everything Is Energy

Everything in this universe is made up of energy. It doesn't matter whether it shows itself as a word, thought, action, element, or object: science has proven that it is all composed of measurable, specific types of energy. Electricity is energy, light is energy, solid matter is energy—patterns of protons, neutrons, and electrons, all vibrating at different frequencies, yet held together by their electromagnetic energy fields.

As humans, we each have an electrical matrix, which is scientifically measurable. We produce between four to fifteen watts of electromagnetic energy, which holds our cells together in a definite pattern, form, and shape. Without this energy, our cells would fall apart. This is true with everything that exists.

Consider this: if everything around and within us is of an energetic nature, our dilemmas, dramas, and traumas also have an energetic source. They are composed of our perceptions of life, residing in the experience held within memory. Our mental perceptions originate in the energy of what we are interpreting, based upon what we have previously experienced. Our conversations are energy. Our diseases are energy. Our words are energy in action.

Taking this concept one step further, we can also learn to work with this energy and change it into something more constructive. We can use this energy to help ourselves in our lives and others in theirs—unless we continue to choose a destructive life by avoiding constructive or selfless choices.

You have the ability to concentrate your awareness and learn to feel these energies, see them, hear them, know them, and then change them. After all, it is only energy. You will learn more about how to do this in future chapters.

I refer to this energy as the language in what we call God that enables it to relate to us and us to it—both being of the same intertwined nature.

II. Synchronicity: The Law of Cause and Effect

We exist on a never-ending continuum of causal moments, followed by the effects of those causal moments, and then by subsequent cause and effect reactions and repercussions.

I define *prayer* as everything that emanates from within us and flows out into the universe. Our every word, thought, and action is our living prayer. Prayer is the energy that determines our life's existence. It comes from within our

Self, and it is the manifestation we choose for ourselves in any given moment. It is a living consciousness in constant action.

Everything we think, say, or do—each prayer—provides a causal moment: that is, it leads more purposefully to the next moment, the next thought, and the next action. Everything that happens is on this continuum—a flow of synchronicity that I call as *the law of cause and effect.*

One time several years ago, a teacher asked me what I thought karma was. I thought for a while and stumbled in guessing based on what I remembered others as saying. He looked at me and said, "Karma is change and nothing more." Over years, I often thought about his answer, and I can see how karma is living motion and nothing more.

The causal moment is a moment in chaos. The next course of activity is undecided. Amidst the chaos is the potential for a greater pattern to come forth. The emergence of this potential depends upon our frame of reference, what we reflect upon, and the life experiences upon which we draw. Any moment, destructive or constructive, is still a causal moment, and we can become aware of it and its potential effect. If we become conscious of our causal moments, we can manipulate and work with them as tools. This becomes easier as we become more conscious of ourselves and less tuned into the dramas and traumas of living. When we concentrate only on self-destructive dramas, our thinking processes become cluttered and distressed. We cannot destroy the memory of previous causal moments, but we can rearrange them by bringing them into a different level of awareness, which is either creative or destructive. Even in the dynamics we think are fate—believing that "we have no choice"—we find that we can transform the experience into a greater wisdom.

We know that for every cause, there is an effect. Everything you have thought, said, and done has made you who you are, what you are, and why you are today. Every thought is a causal moment. Every time you choose, you have an effect on another causal moment. *Once you fully grasp this statement, a new world begins to be opened to you.* You too will see how things have affected you all your life, how everything you have thought, said, and done has made you who you are today.

I would like to suggest that you contemplate each statement in italics below and what it specifically means to you:

You can affect any causal moments in your life.

You have a definite choice about how you want to exist in every aspect of your life and at any given moment.

You can rearrange every moment into something constructive and turn it into something conscious and useful just in witnessing what has transpired—even if it was meant to disturb you.

If we could be totally aware of our own thoughts and experiences for one day or even one hour, we would see just what we are really praying for in each moment.

CONSIDER THE BUTTERFLY

Some time ago I read an analogy by F. David Peat, PhD, author of *Synchronicity*, that I found interesting. It examines the idea that the forces around us are truly connected in a continuum. Here is my summary of his analogy:

In order for the butterfly to come out of its cocoon, it has to gnaw its way out. During that time, thermodynamic forces are subtly at work at the point where the butterfly is using friction to destroy the cocoon. Friction generates heat and deterioration, enabling the butterfly to break free. This movement creates other dynamic forces. Then the butterfly spreads its wings in its new external environment and takes flight. As it flies, as subtle and as light as its wings are, they move the air around it, creating a current in its immediate environment that ripples outward into the atmosphere.

This rippling doesn't stop there but has a creative effect that flows continuously nonstop until it has the potential to affect the entire atmosphere around it in subtle or dramatic ways, just as forces circle outward when a stone is tossed in water.

A stone skips across the water, barely touching the surface. Each time it does, another causal moment takes place. Each ripple is a causal moment that creates subsequent ripples, and so on, into infinity.

This phenomenon can certainly be applied to our own minds and actions. For instance, simply watching an interaction between two people can have lasting effects. Let's use the example of a fight between your parents when you were a child. Perhaps they were arguing, and you were listening to and observing the dynamics. How did you feel? Can you remember how your body was affected by those feelings? Did you feel emotional hurt in your stomach or heart? Do you remember what your other reactions were? Did you try to quell the situation between them, or did you stand back and wish you could disappear? Did you think, "Uh-oh, it's time to avoid Mom or Dad"?

Can you see how the dynamics of cause and effect from previous experiences such as this are still at work in you? Do they apply in some way in your daily interactions? If you had experiences with your parents like those mentioned above, how are your stomach and your heart today? The causal moments from earlier in our lives have resulted in many of the patterns and diseases we have chosen to live with all these years. In other words, most of our emotional, biological, neurological, and physiological patterns have been set in motion by a beginning learned pattern that at one time we accepted.

III. Understanding Self: Seeing and Believing

We often hear, "I'll believe it when I see it." Consider an alternative thought:

It's not necessarily as we see, so we believe, but as we believe, so we see.

What we accept, what we believe, will be.

Our perceptions are based upon our conversations, which in turn are based upon our perceptions. What we "see" is formed from the conversations we have inside and outside of ourselves. These conversations arise from our past causal moments and are expressed in our present thoughts, words, and actions.

To go back to the example of watching parents fight, we might have a current perception that no one ever pays much attention to us, but what we're doing unconsciously is still trying to "disappear" out of fear. Our old belief that being seen might be dangerous for us is the causal moment for being "invisible" to others today. We find ways to disappear through our thoughts and actions. We may act shy, joking around or saying things that diminish our own importance, causing people to ignore us. Or we may develop control issues as defenses. We may even try to gain excess weight in order to "disappear" in the world by causing other people to ignore us. We are powerful cocreators. What we believe will be. We think to create what we think our needs to be.

Beyond our perceptions, there is always more. There is the causal moment. We have reasons for perceiving things the way we do. These reasons come from our self-protection, from inside the walls we have built around us in both our inner and outer environment. We must feel safe in our protected environment before we will venture out into the unexpected. We take one safe step at a time. This is our human nature, not yet fully integrated. But we are learning to become "humans-in-being."

I invite you to go beyond the limits of what you know, beyond the norms that you have been taught and where you have been stuck. Question everything you have learned. Go beyond the perceptions and conversations you have been given from outside yourself. Trust what dwells inside you. There you will find your true Self.

SELF? GOD? THE NAMELESS ONE?

Self. God. Light. Creator. Universal Consciousness. I use these terms interchangeably throughout this book because no one word adequately names the Nameless One.

The Self or God perceived under this definition does not care if you speak in a traditional "holy" manner. Whether you wash your hands with religious intent or attend a church, mosque, or synagogue—whatever you do serves as your way of validating God for you. All modalities of expressing and responding to God serve a purpose. For me, God is beyond religion and religious ritual, although we need these things to help us express the essence of God.

God is within us as a constant knowingness. God is in constant evolution as well—the vehicle for self-expression and self-sustaining life. As we take on that understanding, we can become "so poised, so perfect that none but Self can comprehend," as a prayer of my Order so eloquently states.

Many people think of God as vengeful. I do not perceive God that way. Whatever we want, however we want to be, is all right in the mind of God. There is no god of retribution or guilt. There is no god of sin. This is not the God that I know.

God is within us. We live with God. Self is the living consciousness of God within our bodies—the inner life force and intelligence that guide us in a nonlinear way. Our bodies are simply shells created to allow Self to express through us.

Self has always been there, within us, every moment of our lives, and always will be. We all have this guiding still, small voice within: the representation of a greater consciousness. But some of us have not yet learned how to consciously communicate with it or make it an empowering tool in our lives. I will teach you how to hear that voice within.

At one point, when I wanted to understand more of Self, I sat down and asked the Self within me for a description that I could use to help me explain to others. This was the answer I was given from within:

Self is always there for your guidance and direction. Always there, always waiting. It is always waiting for you to listen. That is why it is here: to guide and direct you back to its Self. Judgment is a human-learned way, not a being way.

Self sees you without judgment. It has no consciousness of judgment or condemnation or consequence. Self sees the truth, but you are never condemned. It does not reprimand or make guilty. It has no personality as you know personality. All have the voice of Self, the inner voice. All living things have this inner voice, an inner constitution of existence. It has no past, no future. It is only in this moment. It speaks to us in the moment, often interpreted as an idea or a thought or a revelation.

Revelation comes from within. Our experiences from wisdom within stimulate our understanding and sight and memory. That is why it is so important to understand Self, to let it do what it needs to do within us and through us, so we can be free to let it be and express itself. When we learn to listen, revelation can allow the Self to reveal the Holy One within. Our old rebellion can shift to a newer, more constructive rebellion, to reveal and revel in change, to take pleasure and express delight in becoming different in our unique way.

How often and how unnecessarily we sabotage ourselves by discounting these interventions, thinking that we are just having a fanciful idea that couldn't be real! "No one could be interested in what I do or what I have to say; they wouldn't believe me anyway." How easily we discount our own experience of Self in the subtle intuitions that are shared with us!

What, then can we trust? Can we trust what we know before another speaks or does something? Have you not experienced this?

Self has no drama or trauma. Self tells us what is. Self is our guidance and our direction, telling us to stand for what we know to be true in the deepest recesses of our hearts. It tells us to trust. And it assumes that we trust and are trusting. We well up with inspiration as Self reminds us that it is the living force, the force we identify as God within us. It is the vehicle for self-expression and self-sustaining life and is in constant evolution with us.

IV. Free Choice or Mass Mind: Which Do You Listen To?

From birth, we are given a choice to use our free will to listen to the guidance and direction of Self or to listen to the world, believing our friends and family and accepting only what we are taught and what they were taught. We can choose to become part of this mass mind, or we can choose Self, refusing to submerge ourselves in the dramas and traumas of our lives or the lives of others.

We can also choose to live in both worlds, integrating the truer spirituality into our lives. After all, isn't that we are here for? We are here to get to know our Self. For me, that means integrating earth and heaven.

Not everything that we learn from the mass mind should be discounted. Mass mind, which is expressed in the world around us, has a place within us. You still need to function in the ordinary world. You need to know how to hold a job, interact with others, and have graceful manners at the dinner table.

But other mass mind concepts tend to negate and sabotage us. They keep us in line with how others think. They do not allow us to get out of the box and consider things differently. Our dramas and traumas are creations of mass mind, which teaches us about retribution, guilt, and sin, but those things don't interest God. The God inside us is not a God of retribution or revenge. God is not saying, "Hmm, I think I will get even with them today," or "You screwed up," or "Uh-oh, you're going to get knocked down three more notches," or even, "You get one more wish today."

Remember, Creator, Self, the God within us, has no pain and no disease; we do. Self doesn't deal in guilt and fear; we do. Self helps us to work with pain and disease as they happen. Self helps us to love and feel the jubilation within ourselves as we recognize it and the joy of limitless giving, forgiving, and living. How can we truly help another to love and have a greater experience of life unless *we* can truly begin to love ourselves?

It is always up to us to choose to listen to the voice of Self. Too often, though, we say to ourselves, "I will listen, but in a moment. Right now, I have to do this or that first." That too is our choice.

SELF TEACHES CONSCIOUS CHOICE

Self teaches that you have a choice in every word, thought, and action. When something is happening to you, stop for a moment. You have a choice to say yes or no to your reaction or creation and the perpetuation of it. You have a choice to get involved and react or to step back, see what is really happening, and decide if you want to react or not. Perhaps you can even change a situation into something greater.

You might not think you have the time to make a choice regarding your reaction or thought, but you do. You can stop at the beginning or even in the middle of any reaction and decide what you want to happen. We can even correct a situation well after the fact, just through integrity and being true and honest with ourselves.

If someone says something to you that would normally hurt you or disrupt your otherwise pleasant day, you can pause for a second and realize that what they said is meaningless. It has nothing to do with you and never has; it only is a trap to get you to be like them. It is only a temporary disconcerting situation, and it is theirs to deal with. This is the way they were brought up. Now you can get back to your lovely day. It's that simple. It's your choice.

Once you start to make these conscious choices, you will find they get easier each time. You can unlearn the way you were taught to think. With practice, you can become more conscious in difficult moments. The very dynamic of being conscious becomes part of your life, and you will no longer need to practice it: it takes over for you. Times of destruction and negation will become fewer and further apart.

You can begin to practice by saying to yourself, "Wait, I don't have to react to this." This inner conversation may feel a bit odd at first, but over time it will become effortless. Consciously apply this understanding for one or two days, then make up your mind to try it for just one more week, and then for the week after that, and so on. As you develop, you will find that you no longer have to keep concentrating on this practice: it will become a natural part of your everyday life. You will let go of many of your old reactive patterns. Without having to work hard at it, you'll have more choices, free will, power, force, and energy. Unconscious reaction will no longer be a part of your norm. You will no longer need to react to the world's destructive activities. Your body will become healthier, responding to your greater choice of health. This act reverberates in the whole body, mind, and spirit, because in reality, there is no separation between them.

In the mind of God, whatever we want is what we get. Whatever we accept is what we have. We are not living our lives chained to fate. We are living examples of what we have accepted into our lives. We have choice, free will. This ability to choose is the carrier of our living prayer.

Many times we say, "Oh no, I've wanted to get out of this neighborhood, and I'm still here." But you are stuck. You haven't learned to reject the patterns and conversations you were taught. You haven't realized that you have taught these patterns as well and are still living, teaching, and reinforcing them in others, because you still believe in them. You are still living in conversations left over from childhood. Ask yourself, "How does that feel?" How does it feel to know that you are teaching your children to negate themselves, just as you learned to do?

For example, a woman might think, "My father was a drinker, and so was every boyfriend I've ever had. Now look: my husband is just the same, and he is abusive too." She has allowed abuse into her life because it has always been a routine part of her thinking and her life. Her children will also carry that learned behavior, as strong as any neural code, because she accepts this as the norm.

If you don't accept what you have been taught, you may be afraid that you won't be loved (as you perceive love). But once you hear the loving Self within speaking to you, you will no longer accept "love" in that old self-destructive form.

Here's another self-conversation: "My father was a mouse, and my mother an overpowering nag. Now look at the woman I married. I married my mother, and I'm now my father." Or, "My dad abused me, and so has every lover and acquaintance I have ever had."

Pay attention to how those conversations feel to you. Objectively and without emotion, re-member (bring the members of your memory back) when they began to happen in your life, and you'll begin to witness the patterns in your life. Observe them objectively, without participation.

Another example: do you tend to act belligerently with others? Think back: did your mom or dad think you were incapable of expressing yourself? Do you also now have some throat, thyroid, lower intestinal, or lung problems? Maybe you weren't able to express yourself before, and now you're fighting back to show the world how worthy you are. You do that with your belligerence, and your body is also fighting back in its own way, trying to give you a way to express yourself. The conversations we hold within ourselves, these perceptions conjured up in our minds, come from and dwell within the mass mind. We then give life to these conversations, and our reactions provide a place for them to dwell in our daily lives, often creating sickness and other distresses. As we participate in these perceptions, we perpetuate this mass mind.

As you begin to understand these things, you will become aware that Self is alive and well. You learn how to reach Self and see all the possibilities that will result. All you have to do is engage with it on a more conscious level. This conscious awareness will lead to life-changing experiences.

You now have the opportunity to stop being stifled by life. We often don't realize that we are stifled because that is how we've been taught to be. This is totally unnecessary. It is only because we have internalized the conversations of mass mind.

V. Hearing Self Speak

The first time I ever heard the Self was on a Sunday afternoon, at a social get-together in 1971. It was a few weeks after I had been accepted by the Order.

Six or seven of us were standing around talking. I noticed one woman standing off to the side. She didn't join in the conversations. She wasn't introduced to me, although everyone else was. I listened, waiting for someone to mention her name. (I don't know why I didn't just go up to her and ask her name.)

Anyway, I was very curious about her. I wondered what her name was, and I was bothered that I didn't know. Later that day, lying down in my own room, I couldn't get her image out of my head. My mind kept thinking about her until I began to doze off to sleep. Just then, from all around me and within me came a clear, booming voice, permeating through my whole being, startling me. The voice said, "Caroline."

"What?" I said, as if someone were standing next to me.

The voice said, "Her name is Caroline."

I jumped up, eyes wide, looking for the person in my room. No one was there. I could not figure out where the voice came from. Then I realized it came from within me. No one could hear what I had been thinking. I hadn't mentioned my curiosity about the woman's name to anyone. I was amazed and felt a wave of excitement wash over me. From somewhere deep within, I was given the answer to my question.

A few days later, I saw one of the fellows who had been at the Sunday gathering and asked him, "By the way, who was that woman who was standing off to the side? You know, the one no one really talked to?"

He replied, "Oh, you must be talking about Caroline."

Over the next several weeks, things started clicking. I began to realize that I could hear what others called Self— the Self I had been learning all about for the past several weeks. I began to slightly understand what Self is, where it is, how to fit it into my life, and how my life was integrated into it. All these small but numerous incidents began to click into an understanding, little pieces at a time.

5

Meditation

Enjoy the silence.
In the silence is stillness.
In the stillness is love.

We seek a greater spirituality
Only because
We see ourselves external to it.
Yet, if we became internalized,
We would not be seeking it
From outside of ourselves.

I. Simple Meditation

Meditation is one of our entryways to the Creator, the Divine Source within, where our healing and intuitive abilities come from. Meditation has been practiced since the days of the cave dwellers. Hunters would learn to sit in the forest for hours, blending in with their surroundings in order to become one with them so as not to disturb the environment and scare away their prey. It took a meditative, concentrated focus to achieve this state.

Since that time, hundreds of different techniques have been developed. The style I work in operates at a deep level. It is an esoteric approach, meaning that it comes from inner teaching. Using it, you will have clarity about what's truly real in your life and all that is available to you.

My style differs from many New Age approaches, most of which don't offer much explanation for what they teach. Many tend to be watered-down versions of what originated as the New Thought movement in the early 1800s. That movement taught parts of the inner teachings, but during the early 1900s, they were diluted to make them more acceptable to the public, which had little background in esoteric thought. These versions were mostly aimed at curiosity seekers and those that wanted to search only partially. At the same time, these teachings came to be regarded as woo-woo or weird. They did little to answer the deepest questions of sincere seekers, and they took people outside of themselves for solutions. At this point, many of these approaches did not reveal the inner teachings of the Self.

But people who awaken spiritually can begin to delve deeper into the inner teachings. My place is to help people go back to the Source instead of relying upon someone else's source or only experiencing what the teachers experience. This latter approach does not do justice to our individual uniqueness. I believe this book guides in a good way, enabling you to get right to Source more directly from within. That Source is Self.

USING YOUR PAST FOR HEALING

Your personality is portrayed in each moment, in your every activity. It pervades your whole constitution, existing in the living consciousness of every single tissue, cell, bone, and muscle in your body. Meditation enables you to see a piece of your personality in a new light. The effects of meditation permeate the depths of your mental and emotional constitution. This same personality, which is alive in us all, is always there and has been with you throughout eons of time.

While doing this inner work, glimpses of your past will show you many aspects of your personality, both in this lifetime and potentially in other, previous forms of your existence. All of them will pertain to who you are now and how your life is unfolding. It will make life easier to be able to understand yourself.

Every experience you have has its origins in another time and place and even beyond that. This includes not only our experiences in this life and previous ones, but all the experiences and beliefs of humankind, which are part of our collective consciousness since the beginnings of time itself. This collective consciousness preceded us and accompanies us, and we carry it with us. It is available to each of us to draw upon and to learn from in our day-to-day situations.

In a meditative state, you can get an objective look at your personality and its conversations. Sitting down, closing your eyes, and asking to see a piece of your past, you may get a glimpse, a flash, a brief memory of something heard, seen, or felt long ago—but it will speak volumes depending on how much you trust your perception and how receptive you allow yourself to be. This revelation will show you some pattern you are enacting in the present, although you will see it in another setting and at another time, when it might have begun. Your awareness of this pattern can take away its power so that you will never be attracted to it again.

You will see that the conversations you had back then are not based on any truth about yourself now, even though you still carry them around. These conversations may have had relevance at another time, but at this point you are no longer the same person. As we observe these older patterns, they change from experience to behaviors to wisdom.

For example, you may have made a mistake long ago for which you couldn't forgive yourself. As a result, today the conversation that directs your life is what a big mistake you are and how unworthy you are. At this point, you can see that this conversation is just a carryover from one choice you made long ago—the causal moment. Looking back at the past scene, you see that your mistake really *was* forgivable; maybe it wasn't even a mistake at all. More importantly, you quickly come to understand that you do not need to live the mistake *now or ever again.*

These realizations flood through your mind, body, and soul. As they do, the process frees you from the pattern that has kept you from knowing your true Self. This moment of recognition may result in a new way of thinking and feeling, physical healing, and many other changes in your life.

There are thousands of examples of this process from my experiences in working with others with healing. The process may be as simple as that of one fellow, James, whose elbow pain disappeared, along with his fear of bike riding, after he called up the memory of falling off his bike at the age of nine. Once he recognized the source of his fear, he no longer needed the elbow pain to remember to be careful and avoid getting hurt.

In some cases, major diseases are healed, or at any rate their symptoms are diminished. People open up to experience more freedom and more love in their lives. Their compulsions and addictions disappear. These are just a few indications of how meditation that shows us the past can be life-changing.

ANOTHER PAST LIFE

The purpose of seeking a past memory is not necessarily to dwell on the past-life experience but to gain understanding of the present synchronicity and how it applies to who you are today. You are given some representation of that past, but the point isn't to go back and try to fix what happened back then. You are living in *this* moment. The particular dilemma, drama, or trauma that occurred may really have been a blessing that led you to communion with your Source. Maybe your soul has presented it now to enable you to work the issue out at a time when you were ready.

Yes, I realize that accidents happen—and that sometimes we are at the right place, but someone comes along that the universe didn't plan on. Maybe the other person was drunk or doing drugs and acted haphazardly in a way that had nothing to do with the soul's plan.

During meditation, you will see things that need to be worked out now, regardless of when they occurred in your past. No matter what it is or where it originated, it is showing up in your life because it needs to be addressed now. From somewhere deep inside, the soul is presenting this repercussion because it knows that you are able to reconcile it with your current life experience.

As soon as you recognize the personality pattern that created the emotional response that you have brought with you from the past into the present, it is no longer hidden, and you can work with it. You realize you learned it from some experience back then (an experience that was also part of the collective consciousness). You took it on years ago, but now you carry the authority to refuse to express it any longer, since it is no longer a real representation of your true Self. You have evolved, and the experience has developed into wisdom.

We all have the ability to access this information from our past years and use it to help us in the present. We can see ourselves back to the beginnings of time. With meditation, if we want to, we can see the composition of the material we are made of—even subatomic particles. Since the time our consciousness began, we have had more than billions of experiences and hundreds of thousands of lives as these dilemmas, dramas, and traumas have manifested in different forms, resulting in who we are, what we are, and why we are in this moment.

New Age teachers speak of reincarnation, although not necessarily as the mystics of old taught it. I speak of reincarnation in the old sense, by which our past goes all the way back to the beginnings of our existence. We still carry these moments and memories of old within us, and we can tap into them to some degree when we are in a meditative state. This goes beyond the usual concept of past-life experience. In a short period of time, you have the potential to receive an understanding of a more whole consciousness. Sometimes it happens in the time it takes to blink an eye. The experience may last for seconds, days, weeks, or months, or it may unfold over time. It depends on what a person needs, not necessarily on what they want it to be.

As you can see, meditation is not active thinking but passive. It is receiving information from a greater source within. As we receive information from current or past times, we do not have to be fearful, because no drama and trauma are associated with it. Self only knows its gentleness. In meditation, you experience nothing in this universe unless you are ready. It's only when we try to crash the gates of heaven that we are likely to experience a shock or trauma.

ASK A QUESTION, GET AN ANSWER

As I was taught, the purpose of meditation is to ask a question and get an answer. It is a path to greater awareness. During meditation, you can ask questions not only about your past but also about other subjects. You can get answers on any subject if it in any way pertains to you and you are sincerely curious or even asking out of innocence. You will get correct answers for your life—or for another's. The living consciousness within us has the ability of understanding and knowing. All we have to do is learn how to tune into that consciousness.

Later in this chapter, I will lead you in a directed meditation to teach the process to you. Once you get the hang of it, you will find that meditation is easy and applicable to every aspect of your life. You can do it even when you are alone for twenty minutes at work or when you are working with yourself or others in healing.

YOUR FIRST EXERCISE: FOCUS ON YOURSELF

Here is an exercise that will give you a chance to explore what happens when you ask a question of your Self. This is an exercise that you can practice often. It may be difficult at first, but you will soon see that it has long-term benefits in your life. Take a moment now to quiet your mind and do the following exercise.

Choose the habit that you *dislike* most about yourself. Keep going back in your mind until you can remember when it started—its initial process, when you first began applying that habit in your life.

Then ask yourself, "Why did it start?" Wait until you remember (which, again, means to bring the members back together). Allow yourself to see, hear, feel, and know what is within you that will reveal your answer. You can then get an understanding of how this particular habit has affected you. You will find yourself reflecting on the current manifestation of this habit in your thinking.

When this happens, turn your attention back to what you just perceived—your first experience with this habit—and watch the situation unfold objectively. Review that dynamic remembrance as if it were the first time you were experiencing it. See if you can find the actual causal moment in your life that led to you to carry the habit with you throughout life, which contributed to who you are, what you are, and why you are today.

If you have found the causal moment, watch what happens as a result of this revelation and your objective examination of it. In that moment, a healing actually takes place, and it will change your life.

Through this process, your transformation has only just begun. It changes your mental perceptions and your emotional reactions to them. It also affects your physical reality, producing biological effects that offset the ones produced by your old thinking processes—illnesses and deterioration you may have been experiencing without necessarily knowing it and which might have led to your death.

This exercise will help to build your ability to watch and perceive your causal moments and understand how to go through your metamorphosis. The idea is to watch the process objectively, without becoming involved in the dramas and traumas you witness. This is not possible unless we try this as a simple exercise and realize that in reality, there is nothing to fear. Nothing will be shown to us that it isn't our concern to know. Nor would these limitations be made visible if to some degree we weren't prepared to see them. The truth does not kill us or do us mental harm; nor can it make us sick. The truth helps us to see ourselves objectively and thereby sets us free.

WHAT MEDITATION BRINGS TO OUR LIVES

When we meditate, we experience many things subconsciously without letting ourselves get in the way. What we experience is in direct relation to what we need. Meditation breaks through layers of intellect, through misconceptions and preconceptions.

Each time you meditate will be different and unique. Although you have done a certain meditation exercise before, your experience will change the next time because you are at a different place of understanding. Through your senses, you may experience a sense of peace. You may experience a sort of dizziness (which I refer to as clarity). You may feel nothing physically. But you will always experience something, either consciously or subconsciously. Self is using this experience as the perfect way to reach you in an unencumbered, gentle manner.

Some people feel out of it when they finish meditating. This is because they are in a different world while meditating, and their body is simply readjusting to itself when they come back.

MEDITATIVE PHRASES TO USE

I have been taught many different meditative phrases, each of which has been purposefully designed to increase insight. These phrases can help us to become more in sync with the Godliness within us. These phrases are truly special. They are alchemical in nature and will help shift you into a more open awareness. They change you through your intent to use them. Mystics used many of these same phrases long ago. Their power perpetuates them throughout history. They are inspirational, which means, "to be inspired to action from within." And I'm sure that some of these can be found in other sources. You may find these phrases helpful in your meditations:

1. Love is inspiring and illuminating; therefore it gives light and life.
2. The Light has a consciousness; it has an intelligence. It knows what to do with me or without me.
3. Every word, every thought, every action is my living prayer.
4. Self is always there, waiting to guide and direct me.

5. Divinity is with me, waiting. I need only to listen.

6. Go forth and heal in love, without judgment.

7. I feel the love of Divinity within me.

8. I know what to do.

9. To see the Divinity in others is the only way.

10. Breathing in the breath of God.

11. I cease to think of God as external. God is within me.

GETTING STARTED WITH MEDITATION

The exercises in this chapter are designed to teach a developmental method that tunes you into your original and personal spiritual mode of perception. These exercises will affect you emotionally, mentally, and physiologically. But before I introduce you to them, I will offer some suggestions about breathing, body positions, and environment, all of which can affect your meditative process.

II. The Breath during Meditation

In the East, people are taught to breathe through their nostrils. In other parts of the world, people are taught to breathe through the mouth. In the West, we bring these two ways of breathing together. We can go through a tremendous spiritual experience when we breathe in through the nostrils, as we did with our first breath at the time of our birth, and breathe out through the mouth, as we do when we express our living words.

I have found that many people on the North American continent find it very difficult to receive answers while in meditation if they are inhaling and exhaling only from their nostrils. In order to receive answers to your questions, it is important to inhale slowly and deeply through your nostrils and exhale softly and slowly from your mouth. Pay no mind to any momentary discomfort. If you practice this breathing, it will become more comfortable. Practice. Practice. Practice. It's really no different than an athlete building a muscle: the more you practice, the stronger the muscle gets.

If you feel constriction in your lungs when you breathe this way, try this: In a slow-motion fashion, breathe in very deeply through your nostrils and expand your chest area at the same time. It may ache and feel tight. Now hold it for the count of ten and let it slowly out.

Do this again, taking a bit of a deeper breath. With each breath, be purposely aware and be sure to breathe in slow motion.

After you have practiced this a few times and gotten it down, bring the breath from your chest into your belly. You'll notice that the breath is able to go deeper and lower into the belly.

It will become easier to breathe this way as your lungs expand through practice, and breathing will become freer and deeper. If you are not used to breathing in this manner, it can be uncomfortable at first, simply because you have forgotten how to do it. With practice, it will become more natural.

THE BREATH OF GOD

Some call breathing in this manner "breathing in the breath of God," because it is God who grants us life, and in this way God is presented to us. As it was written, God breathed through the nostrils of humanity and gives us life.

By breathing in the breath of God, you are experiencing your life source. This is our spiritual side. We can help to develop spiritually through the breath of God. It nourishes us unceasingly. It is our very life's existence. It is a constant reminder that every particle, cell, tissue, vessel, muscle, and bone of our living body in a spiritual sense represents who we are, what we are, and why we are today.

As we exhale out through the mouth, God is expressed through us into word and manifestation. The sound of creation comes forth from the mouth. The more practice and life something is given, the greater its potential and reality.

III. Body Position during Meditation

Everyone has a unique experience of meditation. You will learn to sense your own meditative state and discover how you can best commune and communicate to become one with the Godliness within.

If you want relaxation, you can lie down during meditation. However, I have found that lying down leads to a dreamlike experience. This position is generally not as effective as a sitting position. There's also a greater tendency to fall asleep when lying down. Likewise, although the lotus position may be practical for other types of meditation, it may not be as effective for our purpose.

How we are seated during meditation is important. To get more immediate answers during your meditation, place your feet flat on the floor and sit with the crown of your head reaching into the sky. This promotes greater physical balance, so answers to questions are also more balanced. Make sure you are comfortable and sitting fairly straight.

Sitting is most helpful because the light (the electrical force of the universe) comes from the sun (both living and symbolic) above, and the crown of the head should be closest to and facing this source. At the same time, the feet, planted firmly on the ground, respond to the gravitational pull and activity of the earth. This completes the circuit, creating an optimum environment for attuning ourselves to attain answers. You will have the light, the electrical force, coming in from above and the magnetic force coming up from the earth. As these two elements of energy meet in the center, in the solar plexus, they represent the solar system. This is the place of balance within us. There is a universe within us waiting to be discovered. Only when these two forces come together does the implosion of a whole, greater consciousness occur.

I have personally tried many different sitting positions, with my hands in all sorts of various arrangements. Today I usually sit in a chair with my feet on the ground and my hands positioned so the fingertips are barely touching. Since the pads of our fingers are our terminals for giving and receiving, I can tell when I am in a meditative state because I no longer feel my hands and feet but feel I am grounded and the energy is flowing through my body. I let go of my body in relaxation. I no longer concern myself with the body or feel that it matters. Sometimes I'll even be in a chair with my legs outstretched, my ankles crossed, and my arms crossed and locked over my chest. I figure that God doesn't care. It just wants to share with us.

Your meditation will not be altered by wearing a watch, necklace, or electronic device like a phone. Again, God doesn't care. Things don't matter. What matters is our own dramas and traumas, our conversations that stop the process, that sabotage us.

I teach the position mentioned above to help people break into this type of meditation. Once they get the hang of it, they easily find the position that works best for them.

Get comfortable in whatever position you feel is best for you. Be as relaxed as possible to be ready to receive. Relax and take it easy. Think of it in terms of taking a road trip by car. You're in the start-up period, when you adjust your seat so you will be comfortable traveling a long distance. So get comfortable. Enjoy yourself. No matter how prepared you are, adventure comes as you realize that there is no way you can know what will be shared with you in visual or audial responses.

IV. Music or Silence?

I learned to meditate in total silence. When I began, neither meditation audios nor music appropriate for meditation were available. Nowadays there are tools available to help you in this process. There is nothing wrong with using them as long as they help to stimulate the awareness within so that Self can take over. If the music serves its purpose, after a while you will no longer hear it because you are in a meditative state.

If someone tells you that you need to have a mantra in order to meditate, please remember that mantras were originally created to distract you from thinking during meditation and turn the mind away from its busy, active state to focus on a particular aspect of God. Mantras or chants are tools to help us reach a meditative state of consciousness. They are generally given to you by others. If that took place a long time ago, is the mantra still useful? Furthermore, it is intended to guide you in the direction towards which that tradition wants you to go. Ask yourself, is this still for my best interest, or is it for theirs? In my case, I want to get to the Source directly and simply. I don't want to be distracted by other tools.

The bottom line: use whatever tools are available to give yourself over to the awareness within. The Source is within, and it is more than an exact replica of the Higher Self: it is the same Source.

HOW TO USE THE DIRECTED MEDITATIONS

Read through each directed meditation or exercise in this book several times to get familiar with it, and then try it on your own. You can also ask another person to read the directions aloud while your practice. Another method is to make an audio recording of the directions for yourself and then play it back to help guide you as you practice.

Before you begin to meditate, place a pen and paper near you or on your lap. I often have a writing pad balanced on my lap with a pen in my hand. As soon as I start perceiving something, I will open my eyes slightly, jot down notes, and then gently slip back into the stillness and Mind from whence I receive and see.

V The Experience of Meditation

When we meditate, we are naturally opening our sight to God or Source, and we find ourselves astounded.

Before beginning your meditation, prepare yourself so you can be receptive to what the meditation has to reveal to you. I begin my meditation with a prayer of thanks for what I'm about to receive and then ask about what I want to know, or I find something to say thanks for in order to give glory to the Creator, God, or Divinity.

If you are not used to meditating, you may notice that parts of your body start to feel uncomfortable. That's because you are breaking into a new world, which carries a higher vibratory rate, and your body is readjusting to change. You may experience an uncomfortable feeling right away or after a few days of practicing. You may feel that you have the "shpilkes" (a Yiddish word for jitters), or instead you may feel other bodily sensations. You may even feel calmer and more observant than ever before. Everyone is different.

If you become distracted during meditation, concentrate on your breathing to bring you back to stillness, the place you want to be.

As we begin to work with and develop in meditation even a little bit, the dramas and traumas, the chaotic thinking, the little movies of our lives, dissipate to almost nothing. They don't have much room to exist anymore.

VI. A Focusing Exercise

Read this exercise in its entirety before beginning. Study the text, paying particular attention to what you are looking for as a result of focused breathing. Place a pad of paper and a pen nearby or on your lap. Once you have done the above, you may begin.

In slow motion, imagine yourself breathing in the breath of God. Breathe it all the way in, through your sinus cavities and throughout your skull. Breathe the breath of God in through your nostrils, all the way in, and begin to feel the tingling aliveness of your nerve endings, of everything within you. Feel the alertness, the excitement in your body. The electrical sensation that you may feel is light reacting within your body.

Notice how the bones of your head might feel as the light that you are sensing becomes clearer. You are not really feeling this in the cranial bones themselves, but in the layer of tissue and membrane near the surface, where the nerve endings are located.

Keep your eyes closed and continue breathing.

In slow motion, breathe in deeply through your nostrils, all the way to the bottom of your lungs and down into the lowest part of your belly.

In slow motion, exhale very slowly and fluidly through your mouth. You will feel a sense of flow beginning to happen within you and spread throughout your body.

Observe your body emanating energy. It is generating life force within you. It is your electrical matrix, which keeps all the cells together. Imagine that the tingling is caused by the electrical stimulus in the cells, which may have had a lack of life flowing through them. They are coming alive as the light touches them. Smell the energy as it emanates from you. Keep coming back to sensing the energy. It almost pulses off your body in waves and particles. It's very subtle. Become aware of it. Take note of how it feels in this experience.

Go deeper into yourself. Sense the energy coming off your body. Become consciously aware of what is going on around you and within you. Sense the pulses of energy coming from you.

If you perceive something, slightly open your eyes (or keep them closed if you can) and as briefly as possible, write the perception on your pad of paper. Keep going deeper within yourself. Continue with the breathing; notice if it has changed. Perhaps it has slowed or lessened. It is the breath of God nourishing you and giving you life.

Our senses provide a different experience of what we initially thought were our perceptions. We realize that our previous perceptions, both external and internal, were misconceptions based on, and limited to, things we were taught.

Notice also that a different perception of smell can bring understanding. A memory of something you had forgotten or were unconscious of may come back to you. Observe these memories without allowing them to stay.

Now, with your eyes still closed, slowly scan your body, starting with your feet. Use your internal senses. You will discover areas of discomfort or areas that need work. Slowly work your way up, exploring your body in its entirety. Say to it, "Talk to me. Tell me or show me what you want to show me or tell me." It is not necessary to dwell in any particular place in your body: that often rekindles the drama or trauma and keeps it needlessly alive. The point is to make it conscious and nothing else; otherwise it is like superfluous chatter.

Keep your attention on your body. If you perceive something, write it down. As you scan your body, repeat, "Talk to me. Tell me or show me what you want to show me or tell me." In your mind, listen to the silence and pay attention to the pictures, sounds, feelings, colors, and images that come forth.

Focus on this scanning process while working your way up your body, looking for information as you say, "Talk to me. Tell me or show me what you want to show me or tell me." Practice quickening this process by moving your awareness faster.

Stop at any spot where you feel dysfunction. Keep talking to your Self to gain insight. You will perceive answers in some way—your way.

When you have gone all the way up your body, slowly open your eyes and sit quietly for a few moments. Bring the calmness and peace back with you into your life.

Read what you have written. Does it make sense to you? Does it provide you with a different understanding? Was there a revelation about your life as you looked deeply within yourself?

FOCUS AND PERCEPTIONS IN MEDITATION

In meditation we can focus on a particular place in our body where we are feeling discomfort. We can say to the area of our body which feels the discomfort or pain, "What do you need? What do you want to tell me? What do I need to do?" And it will give us an answer in some way. This is just one way to work with the meditative and contemplative process.

Much of what you perceive from this exercise will be new to you. You are breaking into another world, a greater world of awareness, of consciousness. A seed has been planted. Your life force has expanded within you, possibly for one of the few times in your life. Over the years, we have become logjammed with dilemmas, dramas, and traumas, even from wonderful experiences that we might not have known how to process. Now we are tuning into the Self, which will clean out the cobwebs, rust, and logjams. That is what the light does. This other consciousness is waiting to provide information to you. It never stops guiding and directing us. It is continuously full of information. You perceive only a piece of it at a time.

Occasionally during meditation, you won't remember anything, so the time you spent will seem like a blank. You might think you were asleep, even though you weren't. When this happens, it is sometimes because Self knows when we, in our waking state, would want to take control and get in the way of our learning process. This is what I call playing God with the perceived information. If we are taken out of the way, we are allowing God to be God. Regardless, we are given a lot, even if we are unaware of all that was given. Nothing is really lost!

At other times, an apparent loss of consciousness might have saved us from extreme discomforts, just as when people are given anesthesia before surgery so they don't experience the pain of the procedure, yet when they awaken, the necessary changes have taken place. Even though the body's memory was made unaware of the surgery while it was happening, the etheric memory still retains all that transpired. This is why we sometimes have the psychological and physical aftereffects of the change. Self will always guide, direct, and protect us.

VII. Meditating for Answers

In chapter 10, I have given two longer guided meditations: the Flow of Life and the Divine Self Meditation (the latter formerly known as the egg exercise). They are both ancient exercises, which have been developed to teach us to focus within.

In this section, we will focus on how to get answers through meditation.

HOW THE ANSWERS COME TO US

Meditative answers come in many forms: words, sounds, pictures, and writing—whatever form works best to suit your experiences and needs.

I met a little girl, nine years old, who was at times able to see etheric pictures, words, and other things above other people's heads. Above a person's head she would see what looked like a fortune cookie strip that would state a few words about the other person's world and what they were going through at that point. When the girl's mother, Carol, originally brought her to me, she was in dismay. She did not understand what her daughter was experiencing, although she was freely open to what her daughter was and did not want to taint her ability or impede the gift.

The mother arranged some appointments with me, and together we were able to help the girl to develop her knowing without sabotage from the outer world. Her understanding excels because she is being taught that this is a natural part of our existence and is not to be dismissed. This is one of her tools in life.

Each of us has tools to improve our ability to work with ourselves and others. No one lacks this ability, but if you are aware of it and accept it, you will be able to experience and develop this natural part of your being. Our gifts are made clearer and more alive through the meditative process.

If you are sitting in an exam and need an answer to a question about a text, you can go right to the source, the author (as envisioned in your mind). Begin by closing your eyes and make a statement like this: "Hey, look, Author, help me to understand (fill in the blank). Help me relate to what you've written so that I understand." Then as you take the test, you will get various answers, and they will be correct. It only takes preparation and openness to this process in order to see results.

Many years ago, I worked with a student who tried this technique during a test. The student provided information that came straight from the author but was not in the actual text prepared for the test. His professor asked the student where he got the information, and to avoid further questioning, he replied, "I just knew it, or read it somewhere."

Remember this very important point: you will receive from your meditation and your conscious depth of wonder whatever is necessary for you at any moment. If you need clarification about something you have read in a book, reread the passage a few times, close your eyes, and think about it, wonder about it, contemplate it. Then let it go, and wait. Or you can write the question down in the sky of your mind's eye. When you have it written out, step back in your mind and wait. An answer will come to you. Wait patiently. You won't go without a result or an answer for what you need to know.

This process only works after you have let go of the question and any expectation of an answer. It is a process of waiting without understanding of how the answer will come. The main idea is not to dwell on the question. Often we have to mentally walk away from waiting in order to perceive an answer, either immediately or shortly later. This is the simple process of letting go: let the answers come to you.

With meditation, we take the helm in providing direction and focus for what is within the Universal Mind. Each night, millions of neuronal interactions, firings, and responses within our bodies are working to continue the flow of what we draw from in our experiential life to make way for tomorrow's directions and effects. When we meditate, we achieve some control over these neural events by providing focus and intent.

If you have a specific question or statement you want clarified, your answer will come in the moment, that night, or the next day, but it will be there for you. You just have to ask.

If you are to learn something, you will be told or shown what it is, but only if it is your business or if you have the right to know.

Meditation is a tool to teach us. It is a tool for us to gain understanding of myriad subjects—as long as it is our business to know, and as long as our awareness does not interfere with another person's development. Often I have asked questions about a person and been told, "It's none of your business." Sometimes the Voice within doesn't even bother to answer me. I understand this and don't take it personally. If you need and desire to know something, you will be told or shown what that is according to your understanding of growth and where the soul is taking you in life.

VIII. After Your Meditation

Every time you meditate, it will be a unique experience. It's just like picking up words of wisdom from a great book. Read it once, and you will get something out of it. Read it again, and you will get something else from it as though you had not read it before.

Even if you have done a particular meditation before, you will experience it differently every time, because your understanding grows greater. When we meditate, subconscious experiences go on without interference from everyday conscious thoughts, but what we receive will correlate to what and where we are in life. Meditation breaks through layers of intellect, misconceptions, and preconceptions in unaccustomed ways. For survival, we have learned the way of logical interference, leading to neglect of nonlinear understanding. The logical way is really the difficult way. The easier way is still inherent within us, always waiting, always guiding and directing, waiting for us to rediscover it, our connection to our life, our Source.

At times you might come out of a meditation feeling a little foggy or dizzy. Often you're experiencing a greater clarity that you're not used to—one that is quite separate from the conversations that normally go on in the mind. The foggy or dizzy feeling is a form of resistance that the body and mind are expressing in response to meditation because they are unfamiliar with the state of full realization. Nevertheless, your mental, emotional, and biological constitution is expanding. As you develop in your practice, this foggy or dizzy sense will dissipate, and you will gain many more conscious insights. It is no different from an athlete developing muscles through exercise. The more you use those particular muscles, the stronger they get.

People sometimes describe this dizzy sense after meditating is by saying they feel "out of it." That is because while meditating, they are in a different world of consciousness, and the body is simply readjusting to this world of perception afterward. What they are really feeling is *in* the meditative world. They have entered a new, nonlinear experience within. A shift in their understanding has taken place.

Also keep in mind that no two people have the same experiences. Because of our uniqueness, there are always differences in dynamics and perceptions, even if two or more people get the same answers to a particular question at the same time.

SORTING THROUGH PSYCHIC JUNK MAIL

Many years ago, when I first started meditating, I would get all sorts of visual impressions. Some were normal; some were filled with weird beings and scary images of cataclysmic events. I asked my teacher what was going on. How would I know if these images had meaning for my life or others?

He gave me a technique to use during my meditation that I am now passing on to you. It works very well. Whenever you perceive anything in meditation, whether it is uplifting and inspirational or disgustingly gross and scary, do the following: Before you get carried away into believing this perception, tell it to stand in the Light. Watch it stand in Light, and see what it does. See what the vision becomes; watch it respond. If it's not real, it will dissipate. No darkness, no falseness, no shadow can stand in the Light. No matter how grandiose or revelatory it may seem, if it is not true, it will fade in Light's presence. On the other hand, if a vision is true, not only will it persist, but the Light will make it simpler and clearer.

After you have used this technique for a while, you will come to understand which visions are valid and which are not. You will have your own barometer. Once you have grown accustomed to distinguishing between fact, fancy, and fear, you will be able to immediately sense whether a given perception is truth for you.

The more deeply you wonder about an experience, the greater wisdom will grow you within.

Challenge everything in meditation. Ask for more elaboration or clarification about what you receive. You always have the option to say, "Show me more" or "Tell me more." Keep challenging, keep pushing until all your questions have been answered in their entirety. You will know when you reach this point. Do not rest until you feel fully satisfied with the response. If some perception feels awkward or out of balance, say, "Stand in the Light." Don't be wishy-washy: state this with direction, focus, and intent.

IX. The Retrospection Exercise

This retrospection exercise has helped me to have concentrated focus. Do this exercise when you lie down to go to sleep for the night. It will help to increase your ability to focus.

You can have your eyes closed or open; it doesn't matter. Just bring your attention to what you are doing at that moment, as you're lying there.

Then let your thoughts drift back through your day, remembering one significant event that happened reasonably close to bedtime—anything that left an impression. Perhaps it was a thought that was important to you, or you were involved in some conversation or action that led to a significant outcome. Perhaps it was something you got upset about. You may even have dropped something. Don't get wrapped up in this event. Just pretend you are watching a movie as you are recalling it.

Now recall another significant event that happened just prior to the first one. Then remember something that happened prior to that, working your way all the way back to when you first awakened for that day. At first you may not be able to put things in their exact order, but that doesn't really matter. You will find yourself achieving a more precise order as you practice.

As you practice this exercise night after night, your ability to focus will grow stronger, and you will recall memories you weren't able to remember beforehand.

At the end of the exercise, take everything you saw in retrospect and say, "OK, God, here are all the good things and not-so-good things that happened in my day. Here's the great me and the not-so-great me. Take it all, gather it all together in one lump, and cleanse it for me. Wash it for me, scrub it, reshape it, tweak it, and put it into its place, so I can see how it turns out tomorrow."

Watch what happens with all the feelings you had when you were going through these events. They will be completely different, because the entire essence of the experience will have changed. Every aspect of it will have been purified for you.

Practice this retrospection exercise without telling anyone else what you are doing. It may take ten to twenty minutes to complete at first, but as you continue night after night, you will see how simple and swift it becomes. Events will become clearer and clearer in your mind, and your life will too. Within a couple of weeks, you will be able to proficiently accomplish this exercise in two to five minutes. It is not necessary to work with it more than three to five days a week.

Be objective when doing this exercise. If you become emotional, say, "OK, God, here's another thing: My emotion is interfering here. Wash it, cleanse it, and heal it. Give it back to me when you've done the laundry."

This practice will help you to start each day renewed. It is not a confession of so-called negative events in our lives. It represents all events from one day—all conversations, all significant events from that day, objectively.

Learn to do this. It is a fantastic exercise. It will help to make you more objective and observant. Your memory will improve in amazing ways. You will develop a knowing that will be an important part of you for the rest of your life.

Since we've been talking about a bedtime exercise, I want to also mention that sleep is very regenerative. It is an important part of your growth and development. If you want to take a power nap for five, fifteen, or twenty minutes during the day, do it. It can be very restorative and refreshing, even if you just lie there with the intent of resting without sleep. Just remember not to take the nap too late in the day, or it can interfere with your nighttime sleep pattern.

X. Frequently Asked Questions

Q: Are we supposed to be concentrating on breathing in through the nostrils and out through the mouth just to get into this state, or are we supposed to keep breathing like this the whole time we are meditating?

A: Your intent is to begin the meditation by breathing in through the nostrils and out through the mouth. This type of breathing is conducive to entering a meditative state.

Usually I only use this technique to help me induce meditation; then I breathe naturally. Don't get hung up on how you're breathing unless a gentle reminder comes to you during the meditation. You will find yourself breathing so slightly that you won't even think there is a breath happening in your body. In time, you will even have a sense that you are breathing through your skin.

Q: When I meditate, I feel a tremendous pressure inside my head. What is this?

A: This particular pressure is not necessarily a headache per se. It is a developmental process that happens when you are becoming more aware. It's a sign that your sight is opening up.

Mystics throughout the ages have referred to the eye as sand, which over eons of time evolves into glass. It keeps developing and growing under the pressures and frictions of life's experiences.

You are going through a transforming process. Something is developing within you, and your body is adapting to it—a process that will continue for the rest of your life. You have shown the Self your willingness to go through this change, so the pressure you feel happens automatically. To most, it is a minor discomfort. To some, it's like an internal massage, welcoming and comfortable. If so, enjoy it! This is when the sand is becoming glass, and it is through the glass that we can see.

Q: I saw only black while I was meditating. What does this mean? Is it something bad?

A: This is a big misconception. Many people regard black as bad, something to be feared, and connected with death. Here black represents the fertile ground of the mind of the Creator, where the seed of thought is planted. This is where thought is given its opportunity to be enveloped by the life force to proceed into the world of manifestation.

Q: What should we do with our eyes while they are closed? Do we look up?

A: As you go within, your eyes will go up naturally. This is a natural, automatic process of going within, letting go, and submitting to a greater consciousness within. You should not have to force the eyes to this position; if you do, you are trying to crash the gates of heaven. Don't hurt yourself by forcing anything. It's not possible to crash the gates of heaven.

Q: I have the hardest time sitting still. Why is this?

A: Your body is adapting to a more relaxed state and is not used to it. You have a lot of energy in you that must adjust to this state of stillness. Hang in there. Be observant of these discomforts, but every time you feel them, let them flow away and through you as if they are going down a drain. If the discomfort becomes too great, get up and walk around for a couple of minutes; do the dishes or walk the dog. Then go back to meditation. The sensations of jitters or pins and needles will begin to calm as you practice gently getting up, then going back to the meditation after a while.

Q: I only see colors when I meditate. Is this OK?
A: These colors are serving a purpose. Colors carry consciousness, a vibrational frequency of understanding and perception that carries information. This information is translated into our subconscious for adaptation into a form we can consciously relate to. Colors mean that you are on a stepping stone toward a deeper understanding. The act of perceiving "only colors" will fade after a while, and other impressions will follow.

Our chakras emanate colors, which change every moment according to the experience we are going through. There is always some information in the color or field around people or objects. If you enjoy the colors and focus too much on them, that becomes a trap and limits your growth.

Sometimes I'll witness colors, and sometimes only black-and-white. Sometime I'll notice other beings, who are teaching me. Their life forms may be a pearly gray, clear light, or other colors. Maybe that is the way they are in their world. I try to look at events as interesting, not good or bad, right or wrong.

Q: I get nothing when I meditate.
A: Keep at it. Maybe you really are receiving something, but you are not letting go enough to perceive it consciously. Or maybe you're changing in ways unbeknownst to you in

order to become more conducive to other areas of spirituality. If so, when you're in that place again, objectively ask the Divinity Within if this answer is correct. Also ask, what is meditation developing for you, even though you perceive nothing? Practice, expect nothing else but an answer in some form, and you will begin to see and know more of what is being shown and told to you. Ask your Self about your belief system: do you need other beliefs that might be better or more conducive to thinking and trust for you? Be open for the answers.

Q: When I meditate, I see people I don't know. Who are they? **A:** When this happens, just let it continue to flow. If you are to receive a specific message, you will know. Just keep flowing with whatever you get, but as I've already suggested, at first always challenge these faces or images. Say, "Stand in the Light" with authority and observe them as they do. (There is really nothing to be afraid of: things that are non-linear or ethereal cannot possibly harm you.)

After you have made sure of the image's source by challenging it, you will be able to tell whether it is constructive or destructive to your well-being and psyche. Ask what it has to tell you or share with you. Then you can determine whether to pursue it or not. It is that simple.

6

Intuition, Awareness, and Knowing

Without the recognition of Self love,
How can we truly help another,
To find love, or to feel better?
We must first begin
To love ourselves.

I. Developing Conscious Awareness

The development of your intuitive, meditative, and healing skills requires conscious awareness, that is, being highly attentive to what is going on within and around you. To heighten your intuitive skills, you must be able to control yourself so you can consciously become aware of what is happening within and around you.

EXERCISES IN CONSCIOUS AWARENESS

Try this exercise for one minute.

Sit quietly and think of nothing. Notice all the conversations that are taking place in your mind. Consciously stop yourself from having any of these conversations. Stop being wrapped up in your conversation of your life. Just watch yourself.

Observe your thought process, and examine the situation to see what is really being said and done inside. Then actively think of one particular idea. It is important to establish focus in our thinking, which will enable us to control chaotic thinking and constant chatter instead of letting it control us.

The first time you attempt this exercise, it may be a great success; the next time it might be a total failure. For some, it might be a growing process. You will improve with practice. Again, like an athlete, the more you exercise, the stronger the muscle gets.

Next, watch yourself as another person talks. Try it for just one minute. Concentrate on what is really happening; watch yourself and the situation as if watching a movie. You will notice how busy and active things seem around you; you will also notice the calmness that you are carrying within.

You may think we have no control over what we say or think, but actually we can stop our thoughts in the moment. We can decide what we want to think or say or do. We can change it any time we want to; that is our free will.

Here is another exercise in conscious awareness:

To stop your thoughts, watch what is really being said and done around and within you. Now think of your Self— not the little you, but the big Self that resides inside. Totally surrender to this Self. Love it, and let it know you love it. Feel its constant warmth and flow.

Now watch and feel the scene of this conversation with the Self. You will experience a shift. Knowingly or not, you will be able to tune into a new, more real conscious awareness. With this experience, over time your dramas and traumas will fade away.

Reflect for a moment on your experience with this exercise. What happened for you and to you?

The more often you practice these simple exercises, the greater effect they will have in your life, which has previously been so full of reactions and disappointments. You will begin to experience a relative indifference to the old dramas to which you previously reacted.

Develop the ability to live this exercise in your day-to-day life: With all your heart and soul, feel the love coming forth from within you. Consciously talk to it. Express to it your need to love, and listen as it tells you of its need to love you. Recognize it as a close friend. Become aware of it; you can almost touch it. This is what awareness is. You are taking it on; you are clothing yourself with it. Let it flow through you. Let it live through you. Let it love you and love through you. Feel its love. Let it express its love for you in a way that you have not felt since birth.

II. Awareness Is Your Tool

Here is a story of how I learned to strengthen my ability to be aware and perceive.

In 1974, while I was living in Boston, I was walking downtown with a sister in the Order. We were having a discussion about sight. She was trying to explain to me how we are able to "see" through the act of perceiving. I still didn't understand. She then instructed me to focus on a fellow who was approaching us from less than a block away. She asked me to immediately use my perception and tell her what his life was like.

Before I could tell her that I didn't know how to do this, I found myself perceiving a glimpse and understanding of this man's life and was able to express it aloud to her. I didn't stop expressing what I suddenly "knew" about his life until he was about five feet in front of us. She turned to me and said, "Good!"

That was my first experience with consciously using perception to see. It is a wonderful tool. Remember, Self is never incorrect. Try this exercise yourself. Trust it. Practice it daily.

Awareness becomes your tool. Accept whatever you become aware of. Do not dismiss what this tool is bringing to your attention. If you are having a thought about something or someone, believe in its truth. Even if what you're thinking isn't expressed exactly to perfection, your perception is true—even when the other person denies, doesn't remember, or doesn't understand what you are perceiving.

Use your intuitive awareness. Step out of yourself, perceive what is going on around and within you, and trust it. Continue with what you were doing or saying, but watch what is happening. Hone this tool; make it a strong presence in your conscious life. Practice to make it more and more accurate. The more you do this, the more your resistance to accepting your insights will diminish. Be in that consciousness as totally as you can. Be in the Godliness that is giving itself to you. Get yourself out of the way. Keep practicing. Do you understand the importance of practice by now?

Talk to this consciousness as if to a close friend. It will have more to give you as you become more comfortable with it, and you will pick up more insight and knowing. You will get impressions. Don't ignore or dismiss them. You are now open to these things.

III. Conscious Prayer

Everything I teach is based on prayer because it manifests in results. But the results are due to our conscious awareness and intentions. I am continually conscious of being in prayer most of the time. Earlier in the book, I described my understanding of the concept of prayer. I want to repeat it here because it is so important:

As you think, so you are. Every word, every thought, every action is your living prayer.

We pray in three ways: vocally, through our words; mentally, through our perceptions and thoughts; and actively, through our intentional actions. Our thoughts and prayers are made manifest. What we want is what we get. There is an expression: "Be careful what you wish for; you might just get it." Think about this. Is it true in your experience? Can you relate to it?

In my experience, I welcome what I pray for, the manifestations and answers to my prayers. They help me to understand more every day. They are also my proof that the Creator, God, is alive and well within me.

We can pray either to negate or affirm something. Everything is prayer, and we have free choice as to how we utilize our prayers. Nonetheless, if someone tells you they wish ill for you, it will not manifest unless you choose to believe them and accept this prayer consciously or subconsciously (even in a moment of fear). You have the choice not to accept anything of this nature. Isn't that a great thing to know?

WHAT YOU ACCEPT IS WHAT YOU GET

Mass mind is what we've learned in life—what we were born *into*, but not born *from*. Its basis is fear and mistrust, and its purpose is to keep you as a controlled part of itself. Until now, you have been taught that as long as you believe what everyone else believes, you can feel a sense of belonging with the rest of the population and your environment. In fact, mass mind is keeping you from the truth—a truth that is *not* based on fear and mistrust, but on faith and knowing.

For example, the mass mind understanding of the ego is that it gives us personal glorification and that this personal glorification is bad. Many New Agers in particular think that we should get rid of the ego because they believe it blocks our ability in some way; therefore we must destroy it.

My understanding is that the ego is a necessary part of us. It is the vehicle for externally expressing the Divine movement within. It makes us feel strong, confident, and secure in our world, even though it can be perverted into arrogance—a distortion of our Divine expression.

The ego is not the cause of our inability or reluctance to let go of problem issues within us. Rather, as I have mentioned repeatedly, there are *causal events* that precipitated the distress in our lives. We cannot blame the ego; we must look to those past events that caused it to swell or diminish. This must be clearly understood: the ego has a purpose and function. It is to allow, with humility, the Godliness within us to express itself for its own glorification. What we call *ego* would not be there in the first place if it did not have a function. We are the ones that distort its function of intent—not the Devil or the Evil One. We have free will and consciousness. Without the ego, we would be like an old pair of worn-out shoes.

IV. Everything Happens for a Purpose

Everything that happens in our life happens for a purpose. Everything is OK. Everything is a stepping stone in synergetic, ongoing activity and flow.

Once when I was in Fort Worth, I was walking in Cow Town, an older area known for its slaughterhouses. The streets were mostly empty. I was walking with another brother in the Order. We were walking on the sidewalk, which was fairly wide, along a block filled with closed storefronts. The sidewalk intersected with a very odd-looking alley. I knew from walking in this neighborhood before that there was nothing in this alley, not even garbage cans or boxes against the walls. Further back about fifty feet, there were two or three rear doors to shops. There were no windows, no other exits at all—just an empty alley. There were two blank brick walls on both sides, and another wall on the back, forming the enclosure. There was only one way out: on the street side. As I said, it was an odd alley.

Before we reached the intersection of sidewalk and alley, we saw a tall, emaciated street bum standing by a parking meter next to the alley entrance. He looked down as we started to get close to where he was standing. As I glanced at him, I noticed that his face was covered with oozing cuts, as if a razor had been taken to his face. His glazed eyes were tinted yellow. His clothing was oily, dirty, and tattered. I walked up to him and said, "Oh my God, you're hurt! Can I help you?"

My friend kept saying, "Let's get out of here. Let's go!"

I said, "No!" I repeated my request to let me help him; the man looked into my eyes expressionlessly and didn't answer me. I asked again, and he finally responded by simply shaking his head: "No."

I insisted that he let me help him. I said, "I'm going to help you!" The cuts on his face were awful. So I stretched my hands outward toward his face to heal them. Before I was able to touch his face, he backed away and quickly moved into the alley only four feet away, behind the sharp corner of the building.

Within seconds after the bum disappeared from view, we heard a most unnerving sound coming from the alley. It was a high-pitched scream, but it wasn't like a human scream; it was much higher than I thought a human voice could possibly reach. The two of us bolted to the corner to look in the alley, but the fellow was not there.

Over many weeks, I wondered what the experience was really about. Over time I also realized that this was a learning experience for me and might have been a test. I know that everything is put in front of us as a stepping stone for our growth. There is nothing to be afraid of: no darkness, no shadow can stand in the light. None. This was one lesson I took with me from this experience.

7

Understanding Healing

Just as we cannot destroy matter,
But only rearrange the molecular structure,
So it is with our memories.
We cannot destroy our memories,
But we can rearrange them
To reveal a greater understanding.

Healing is simply this: By utilizing our Divine Self and by allowing it to utilize us, we focus our inner sight on a particular topic to help it to realize its perfection. We can get ourselves out of the way just enough to see through the knowing of Self. We can also recreate what is before us into a newer and greater consciousness. We recreate it in the image of the Self. Using light in its energetic form as our tool, we take the negative energies and shift them into a more positive, focused, and productive form of energetic response.

After this point, when referring to energy, I am referring to what are called *morphic fields*: the field of intangible receivers and transmitters of stored information that extend forth from our being.

In this chapter, you will learn more about how to experience and work with morphic fields. We can initiate, create, manipulate, and manifest the information expressed in these fields. Therefore every one of us has the ability to generate healing in ourselves and others.

In this chapter, I am presenting both simple and advanced healing techniques and exercises to aid in your developing awareness of the energy in light. Some of these exercises have been used for thousands of years and have influenced humankind in evolution and the developmental process of finding Self within. I will help you move more deeply into the world of healing. As we go further into this book, you'll find that *light* also refers to the understanding of *intuition*.

All the gifts need light to function: no gift can be without it.

Through these exercises, you will gain useful information that will enable you to realize your source of energy and its causes and effects, which can be directed into either a creative or a destructive way of living. You will gain knowledge of your individual source of insight and learn how to use its energy not only for healing yourself, but for the benefit of others as well (if this is your goal).

I. Introduction to Healing

We're going to talk about imagination and how to use visualization to create something newer or greater. In order to do this, first we have to see it in its perfection—the way we believe it's supposed to be in its final, perfect form. If we cannot visualize healing, it is simply not going to manifest.

Purposeful focus can easily be developed, and it's a must for purposeful living. The greater Mind takes what we have created through our imagination and reshapes, molds, kneads, and purifies it into something more valuable for the people and situation.

Our worldly priorities and diversions have largely degraded our abilities for purposeful manifestation. As we begin to recognize this fact, these destructive diversions drop away, making it is easy to reestablish our connection with Source and all that it has to offer us.

Nothing is really new; it's just been further developed.

At some point, someone actually invented the chair! For two million years, humans sat on the ground, tree stumps, and boulders. Finally, someone saw that they could carve a tree stump into a form that they could carry with them. Then another, lazier person, who wanted more convenience, wanted it to be more comfortable and added arms, and another added a back rest. Thousands of years later, someone else came along and added wheels to make a rolling chair. In our modern society, someone else added a stereo, and another added heating elements and vibration.

Take a look at everything around you and reflect on its developmental stages. Everything is developing from what it was before into something more. As a result, there really is nothing new in this universe. From this perspective, we can also understand that tomorrow doesn't exist, except as we know or imagine it to be *now and based on previous experience.*

Healing comes from seeing beyond the limitations of what we have already known and experienced. Healing is realizing, knowing, and accepting the highest potential for ourselves as it patiently awaits us. This leads to wisdom.

To work with healing is seeing, a kind of premonition— what the Self sees and knows to be true. This is the moment when, through free will, we can choose to pursue the idea. If we choose not to, there is no punishment. Our soul is always setting us up for evolution. It is always presenting us with ways to work something out that enables us to go forward in knowing our Self.

In our life, we have been taught to settle for what is, what has been shown to be. But we do not have to continue to accept these things. Thoughts that are accepted as the norm are only the beginning of what can be. We can go beyond resistances, dilemmas, dramas, and traumas. We can be open to the synchronic flow of life and recreate it to have greater potential than has been shown to us already. *It takes a newer idea for greater understanding, illumination, and livingness.*

Once we become aware of this possibility, we become greater participants in the synchronic flow of life and a greater awareness of spirituality. Many people are already beginning to become aware of this potential and grasp this dynamic concept. They are also just beginning to step out toward the possibility that we may actually be cocreators of reality.

As long as we live within the limitations, the denials of our understanding and accept those limitations, we cannot be healed or have greater access to spiritual gifts. It is our goal to search for, find, and release the limitations that are ingrained in us so we can be freer and have access to healing and the gifts that are waiting to be discovered.

HOW TO IMAGINE AND REALIZE A GOAL

We now know that we have the ability to imagine and create a greater thought, a better way of doing something. We can also use this ability to help someone feel better. Once we have created an image in action (seeing something in what we think is its perfect form), we can let go of it by turning it over to our Source. Once we tap into our Self to reform an old, limiting concept, we are shown how to achieve this visualized image by allowing the Self to guide and direct us. Often all of this is shared with us without our knowing it.

Self speaks to us in words, sensory perceptions, and images. We can get an idea from Self of the final, perfect form of a thing. This idea is like a point of light made manifest within the depths of blackness, the breeding ground of Godliness within us. This is where all things first manifest: in the rich soil of the mind of the Creator. This light is a seed planted in the soil. Like that seed, it carries a world of information for us to draw upon as it develops and flourishes. This information arises from sources embedded within our experience and wisdom, giving us a pattern to draw upon.

Often, just as you are focusing on something, thinking about how to make it better, an idea will come to you. It feels like inspiration—the aha! moment that we have all experienced at various times. If we are willing to see beyond our limitations, we can experience this idea formation even in ordinary events.

I began to be able to wake myself up two minutes before my alarm rang, then ten minutes before the alarm, or at any time I wanted. The only ingredient I needed was desire from the deepest recesses of the heart.

Healing comes through this same potentiating force of the Self within. If someone comes to us with a cut, we can close our eyes, hold our hands over the wound, and "see" our fingers extending into the tissue, releasing the shock and bringing the sides of the wound together to become one and whole again. The more you practice accepting the potential of this force, the more effective you will become.

Every one of us has a unique capacity for working with healing. Everyone has a different personality and a different way to utilize the healing energy and light that shine from within. You will learn which way is your way, as there is an aspect of healing energy and/or light that is your unique style of knowing.

Remember, we have the ability to consciously recreate something greater.

Keep this in mind. It bears repeating. It is one of the greatest keys to understanding our existence and our purpose. It is also one of the greatest keys for connecting with and becoming more conscious of our Source.

SELF: THE INTUITIVE SOURCE

Sometimes we will get an idea from Self, but then we think, "Oh! I've got it!" and we claim it as though we were the ones who came up with it. But intuition means inner teaching. It wasn't us: the idea was shared with us before we knew it. Our unique and individual Self presented the idea to us in the aha moment. The intelligence of our inner sight showed us what something will look like in its ideal form. This is our golden opportunity to acknowledge Self. We haven't yet seen the thought manifested in solid form, but we see it inside as an impression and an image. The idea will become manifested in form as we step out into what Self has shown us and let go of superfluous thinking or inner conversation.

If we create something on our own, its physical manifestation is not, and never could be, its actual perfection, but only our image of perfection. We may try to get to the closest point of perfection, yet we will fall short. Only Self knows the true image of perfection. We must trust this knowing and follow its lead as if we were blind, seeking its support and help. The idea here is to learn to be more objective and observant. This takes practice, practice, and more practice.

In this way, we have inner sight and we truly are cocreators in the image of the Divine.

II. The Law and the Truth in Action

A person does not heal himself or herself or anyone else. There are universal laws at work within the healing process. The Divinity Within always expresses itself us through the laws of creation. Healing comes from the law of manifestation. Divine Self expresses the truth of this law within us. As we begin to trust and accept that the Self innately knows what it is doing, it begins to have an effect in our lives, the lives of others, and situations that we focus on. Our role is to get out of the way and allow this to happen. We must allow the power, force, and energy of the Divine to take over. Once we intentionally give way to its direction, it knows what to do without our interference.

Trust the law and the truth of healing manifestation. Trust that the Divinity, this Divine Consciousness, is alive and well within you and with you. We all have this Voice within us, every moment of our lives. It is the light that is alive. Self has consciousness, and it has intelligence.

WHAT WE ACCEPT, WE GET

Every thought is a causal moment, either consciously or subconsciously, which leads to an effect. This is the law of cause and effect: for every action (or thought) there is an equal and opposite reaction. What you reap is what you have sown. What you perceive is what you exemplify and receive.

This law of cause and effect was discussed earlier in this book, but it is so important that it bears further elaboration. Here are a couple of simple examples: Remember the times when you were walking down a street, focusing on some thought, when all of a sudden you turned around because you thought or felt someone or something was right behind you? When you turned around, you found a person staring at you from some distance away. Or you had a concentrated thought of something you deeply desired, and then something different took your thinking to another topic. Soon afterward, you were walking down the street and saw the exact object of your desire in a store window right in front of you. Or perhaps someone was holding the item.

When these things happen, you are picking up on a vibrational pattern, a frequency. It's a signal of focused intent to the Universal Mind. It's a prayer, and that prayer was answered. These are simple variations on ways we tap into and utilize cause and effect.

Another aspect of cause and effect is thinking in a destructive manner. As we develop dislikes or negative opinions, we turn them into destructive behavior. As we develop those patterns, they become a part of our lives: "No one likes me. No one cares about me. Everyone has more than me. I'll never get anywhere in life. I'll never move from here; I'm stuck here because my mother and father lived here, and their parents before them."

Science has proven that our thoughts create a physical, energetic response and can produce activity that can be measured with proper instrumentation. We are like a camera that is taking a picture. That impression has the potential to manifest, mentally, emotionally, physically, or in combinations of these.

There are even some people who, while using an actual camera, can mentally visualize an image that is not even in front of them, and this image will the appears on the film negative when it is developed.

This being true, we can proceed to the next level of thought: if we are working on someone in healing, we can hold an impression of what we perceive as perfection, and that person will be affected by this impression.

THE LAW OF CAUSE AND EFFECT IS A CONSTANT

You will find all sorts of applications of this law, not only with healing but in your everyday life. Pay attention to what you are thinking; then look around and pay attention to what you encounter next and what you are attracting. Don't you often run into or hear from the exact person you are trying to avoid? Don't you sometimes ponder on the joys or sorrows of an event that could happen to you and then have the same or a similar event occur in some form? Don't you frequently hear from the person you were just thinking about?

There are endless applications of this principle in action. What are you thinking? How does that relate to what happens next? What happens after that? It's a continuum. This concept is really no different from a butterfly taking flight and forcing the air currents air to move in a different direction around it.

Learn to trust your objectivity. Reread and become more aware of these principles, and watch objectively for their effects. These cause and effect relationships occur constantly. The more we are aware of them, the more we can utilize them in preparing and controlling ourselves. Our thoughts and actions reflect and affect our immediate world as well as the world around us and all the generations of people to come. Isn't that exciting?

Take the gesture of waving to someone to say hello. In ancient times, the right hand was used for blessing someone approaching or leaving. So when you hold up your right hand to say hello, you are, historically speaking, asking a blessing for that person. This may be just a reflexive action, yet it is a pattern established by an ancient ritual that has been passed down through the generations. This ritual is being reenacted every day. The person you are waving to, without any realization on their part, will feel something that they may not be able to even express but was initiated many generations earlier. You both feel a sense of union in camaraderie, which is the effect of that ancient causal moment.

TUNE INTO YOUR INTUITION

These universal laws of manifestation, of cause and effect, are demonstrated in our intuition. We can tune into ourselves, build awareness, and use our intuition within any given moment. Think of the times when people approach you: even though they do not express it, you know they feel good and safe with you; they trust you and want to share with you. You may even be able to perceive what they are going through at that moment. By using your intuition, you can see what has happened in their lives to create what you see. You will be able to see their dramas and traumas, their sadness, joy, pain, or whatever else is on their mind. You can sense it through the pictures you receive from them, right there in the moment.

Realize that your perceptions are correct. If you share those perceptions with these people, they might admit what you confront them with, but only if their feeling and thinking aren't fear-based. If their constitution is based on fear and they are trying to fool themselves and the world, feeling internally threatened, they won't admit the truth of your perceptions. Either way, trust your perceptions. The more you practice paying attention to others, the more you will be able to pick up and understand what is going on within and around you.

These intuitive perceptions actually happen with everyone, but they can be sabotaged by certain beliefs, such as, "I choose not to acknowledge these events and perceptions, because I think I'll have to change in some way. I just don't have the time to do this now." Events happen in our life, and conversations happen in our mind. The thinking mind is planning, interruptions occur, and we have control issues that we're dealing with.

You can learn to apply this intuitive use of the law throughout your life.

III. The Genetic Code

Since the beginning of time, our soul has always been seeking new experiences in order to evolve. Our history, our path of experience, and the patterns that we have accepted help us to feel more comfortable with life's experiences. The soul is always presenting to us what we need in order to evolve. There is nothing too little or too much for us to handle. We get to say, "This is not the experience I choose or want. I didn't ask for this, and I don't need it." The soul is amenable to our search for guidance at any moment.

Every experience is stored in the fluids and tissue of our body memory. Every experience is transmitted to the neural receptors in our bodies and is then embedded into memory. The firing of the neurons and the synaptic response carry this information, which is potentially expressed in our thoughts and bodily responses as well as larger behavioral patterns.

These responses continue at night, and each one shapes a little piece of our experiences from that moment onward, into the next day and for the rest of our lives. Of course, the pathways keep changing and adapting each moment in response to each event. Nevertheless, we have free will, which can disrupt these setup patterns.

Although accidents can and do occur, the soul knows how to redirect your entire life to enable you to work on what is important for your growth and evolution in self-knowledge.

Neurological activity during sleep draws upon our previous experiences to form patterns for future responses, which are in constant readjustment. A network of ideas emerges, creating a number of possible pathways to be followed in events yet to occur. The more things we have going on in our lives, the more patterns will be created in our perceptions, responses, actions, and interactions. Through our free will, we can consciously perceive the patterns that formed while we were asleep and we can determine which path we will take. We can see the potential damage in a given course of action and take control by changing our mind and saying, "No! I'm not going to allow this to happen to me!"

As we learn to focus more consciously, we can hear our thoughts and see the direction we are heading in; we can also see which thoughts we are discounting and which we are paying attention to. This might make us more aware of what has the potential to happen next. This warrants further explanation, as it is a vital part of understanding our ability to heal ourselves and others.

We are physically made of electrical impulses generated by particles, which are gathered into a concentrated, semidense, formed mass called a *wave*. This is what develops into and gives us form. This mass also has electrically charged emanations that carry the intent of constant information that we have recreated from our conversations and perceptions of experiences and the things that are taught to us in our subconscious mind.

These emanations of intent carry a pattern. This is the substance of the consciousness that manifests in our world and the atmosphere around us; it influences the universe as patterns that are set up for the next event to occur. This ethereal, nonlinear substance manifests as linear substance and activity.

IV. The Origins of Disease

All emotional trauma from the past is held in the body's cells in the form of energy. The trauma is the creation of the diseased body. It starts with our mental perceptions, proceeding into our emotional response to these perceptions, and thence into the physical body.

Whether you participate actively or merely observe any event, you take it in, and it affects you first with mental reinforcement and then emotionally. We may not be sure at first how to react, but then we determine how we are supposed to feel and what we should do about it. If the event is painful, we might cry or feel hurt. Every time a similar situation subsequently occurs, that reaction is repeated and eventually becomes an ingrained memory. In this ingrained memory, the reaction becomes a internal pattern affecting every aspect of our lives and becoming a part of our personality and behavior. Perhaps we learned that we should not cry lest we be yelled at, hit, or mocked. Perhaps we learned that we are owed much more than the world gives us. Whatever we learned, it carries through and into every aspect of our lives.

In the next step, these reactions bleed into us on a biological level, beginning to manifest as psychological disease. These responses may lead to emotional discord such as fear or hate, resulting in ulcers, cancer, or other bodily dysfunctions. If we continue to ignore the lessons to be learned, these memories eventually manifest as disease.

Emotional traumas and shocks from the past are held in the cells of the body. This phenomenon is what we are sensing when we are working to heal another person; we feel it in the form of energy. In healing, we work with this energy to release this trauma. We must wait until we feel the flow of its release. Once it is complete, the old patterns diminish and life changes and shifts in consciousness. If you are working on another person, the other person may or may not feel the change at first. You must trust that it is complete based on your experience in feeling the area of shock trauma and witnessing its release.

WHAT IS DISEASE?

Many diseases are nothing but mental pictures to be eradicated by clear thinking. Very few diseases are inherited. Most people are introduced to them between the ages of one through seven, or in the prebirth or birthing process.

For example, if a baby is delivered by metal forceps or pulled from the birthing canal with suction on the head, this changes its cranial rhythm, creating a strain—possibly cranial bleeding, stress, and irritation—that can affect the child for much of its life. Those who understand the spiritual-psychical world of healing can repair most of this damage and spare such people unnecessary physiological and emotional dramas and traumas.

I have worked with many people who came to me with cranial or asthmatic conditions as well as lung, throat, jaw, and mouth problems. Through my work, I have found that most of these people had clamps or forceps used during the birthing process. They might not have been properly treated, so that not enough air was allowed to come forth to create their first cry. Many of the people I have worked on have checked this out with their mothers or other family members who were present at their birth. In these conditions, we can help to create a flow of life force in the lungs that will help this condition.

Others with asthmatic conditions have had their breath taken from them in shock or dismay and subsequently developed breathing, throat, or lung distresses. We can also work with these individuals and help them to feel better.

Events that happen in our lives remain in our cellular memory. Our subjective reactions to unhappy events, such as death, divorce, discontent and other troubles, manifest on a biological and physiological level, and eventually our health begins to suffer. We feel the effects of these things as a lack of ease: disease.

Disease results from not knowing or understanding our true nature. You do not have to accept disease, even contagious disease, in your life. In fact, contagious disease surrounds a person with an aura of magnetic atmosphere that can be broken down and worked with in healing.

You can focus your attention and concentration to sense healing according to your own unique ability. In my Spiritual Healing workshops, I teach participants what the power, force, and energy of this consciousness can accomplish in the world around us.

In the next section, you will be presented with several exercises to help you focus on spiritual healing, and you will learn how it feels for you. You might get a greater understanding of your own unique ability.

V. Realize Your Place in Healing

We are living healers. We carry this ability with us wherever we go, even when sleeping; you simply have to become more conscious of it. You don't have to let everyone know, but you can tell someone who is in need that you can help.

When we are working with healing, it is our place to listen to another in humility; in fact, it is our place to listen at all times. You can learn to listen in an objective way, without participating in someone else's reaction while showing that you can comprehend their distress. You will be able to see results just from your listening. This alone will help you and others to achieve greater stability. When you listen with objectivity, your very silence could be helpful or could bring an answer in some form. As you are listening to someone else, you can help them to disassociate from the problem, allowing them to realize that at any moment they can choose again. As a result, for a few minutes or even much longer, the other person will no longer be in their particular dilemma. Help them make another choice.

You can use your abilities anytime you want. If you don't use them all the time, don't feel guilty: these abilities lay dormant until the time when you will use them. That becomes your next practice time. Everything is practice. When you are in a learning mode, you can always continue to grow.

Some will approach you in a hostile or negative way. Knowingly or unknowingly, their only purpose is to throw you off balance and sabotage you. They can only succeed if you allow it to happen. An easy theory to understand, yet it takes practice to master!

It is not your job to heal the world, and it is not necessarily your place to work with everyone you meet. You may not be the right person to work with a given individual. They may not need your help. Someone else may be more suited to fill that person's needs than you are. This is absolutely fine. There are all kinds of avenues for healing.

Today's world is much more accepting of healing than it was even five years ago. It will continue to grow in acceptance. If someone is interested in what you have to offer, go for it!

VI. Using Your Many Senses: The Energetics of Light

Magnetic energy flows across the body. This flow of energy follows the heat cycle or movement of the life force within us. If we become still and go within ourselves, we can feel the pulse of the flow of this cycle. When I am working with someone, one of my own indicators is feeling this flow. When I feel the flow moving freely, I know the healing for that specific area is completed (at least on my part). The other person may feel the effects either immediately or over time, as needed, but I know the seed has been planted and fertilized, and now it will start to develop. The recipient might need a reminder of this healing every now and then depending on the amount of sabotage he or she experiences. Reminding the recipient will reinforce the healing and help to change the situation.

Following are several healing concentration exercises that will help you realize what you are feeling when tuned into the magnetic energy of a body. Some require the use of a partner. Be quiet, be still, and focus on the love in your heart. This will help you to tune in to what you experience.

Remember to gently breathe in through your nose and out gently through your mouth. You are breathing in the breath of God. Concentrate on your breathing, and notice a change in how you feel. You will feel a sensation in your head and experience a clarity you did not have before. This simple act of concentration on your breathing can create productive changes which will stay with you and develop for the rest of your life. This is an ongoing and evolving exercise. It will place you in a receptive state so that you can be used to help yourself and others to heal.

THE GROUNDING EXERCISE

In this exercise, you will practice experiencing what healing energy feels like to you. This exercise happens to be helpful for those with mild to moderate dyslexia and hypoglycemia. It is also good for calming an emotionally chaotic or overstimulated state—what I sometimes refer to as a bombarded mind. On many occasions, I've seen it relieve people of their feelings of chaos and confusion. When I teach this exercise in my workshops, people are better able to understand what energy and light feel like.

The pads of our fingers act as terminals, which both transmit and receive a current. The first three fingers—the thumb, forefinger, and middle finger—carry the greatest current. You can feel through the fingertips. A lot of nerve endings are located here for that purpose.

The left hand is a receiver. The right hand is a transmitter. The same holds true even for left-handed people. (But if you should prefer to use the left hand, God is not going to look down on you and say, "Sorry, wrong hand; can't help you until you change hands.") The right hand is the giving hand, as in the historical transmission of blessing in waving goodbye; the left hand receives.

In this exercise, take your right hand and hold the first two fingers about an inch to an inch and a half apart. Gently place them an inch to an inch and a half above the eyebrows, one finger above each eyebrow. You'll notice two slight indentations on your forehead where the fingers seem to naturally fit. Lightly touch your forehead with these fingers. If you leave them there for a little while, you will begin to feel a slight sensation in your fingers and/or in your head, which will build up and then disperse. You are dispersing chaotic energy and throwing the current into a balanced flow so that the body and brain and mind can operate more smoothly. The effect you get depends on your needs at that moment. Sometimes it takes five seconds to complete, sometimes a little longer. You can do this anytime, anywhere. I have heard from many people how effective this exercise is.

Remember to just barely touch the area above the eyebrows with your fingers. The sensation you feel is the stimulation of a neurological response. Again, it's great for the mildly dyslexic person, or if you are burning out at home or work and you feel you can't handle things very well. It works almost like an ignition and may feel like the flickering of a candle.

This exercise stimulates an area inside the frontal lobe area of your skull generating into the center of your head between the pituitary and pineal glands. Esoterically, the space between them is seen as an arc of light. People will naturally feel much better when this arc is functioning at its natural capacity. A spark of life is there. In a fully functioning human being, that arc is fully ignited. If it is weak or hardly detectable (as in some people that I've worked with), the person is listless, deteriorating, or hardly alive. Some are on the verge of passing. A fluctuating or sputtering arc reduces emotional and physical functions.

THE FIVE-FINGER EXERCISE

This is a simple exercise that allows us to feel the energy, the light, and the presence of the Divinity Within.

Again, as you begin, your hands and fingers will be barely touching. There is no need to rub your hands together to generate an electrical charge. Simply place the five fingers from each hand together in a kind of tent. Your hands can be up or down—whatever is comfortable for you—but don't let them touch silk or wool, because that will create an unnecessary electrical discharge and diminish the effect of the exercise. Don't press your fingers together; just barely touch the fingers and hold them there. Then hold this position until you feel the full effect.

You'll notice a feeling of heat or vibration between the palms, even if you have cold hands. Notice how it begins to build. It will increase. The palms will begin to tingle a little bit, and more life force will flow into the blood. Actually, you are assisting the life force and its flow. Wait in that position until you feel the flow in your fingers or your hands.

This exercise not only promotes a greater neural flow but also improves the flow of the life force through you. This will affect your day and your entire life. Although this practice will affect your blood pressure, what you are feeling is not because of a blood pressure change.

This exercise will help during the day if you are not feeling well, or if you are shaking or feeling a lot of chaos in your day: it will help eliminate these conditions, and you will feel better inside. Do this exercise if you feel stuffiness in your head; it will diminish some of the sickness you might be coming down with. This practice can even be helpful when you are unable to take your prescribed medications for several hours. This is an easy exercise, and very beneficial for everyone.

AN ENERGY STABILIZING EXERCISE

This exercise needs to be done in slow motion—not quickly. You will need a partner.

Stand facing each other. Take hold of your partner's hands. Cross your arms so you are holding their right hand with your right hand and their left hand with your left hand. Relax and close your eyes. Breathe in very slowly. Breathe in through your nose all the way down to your belly and gently and slowly out through your mouth. No heavy breathing. No hyperventilating. Slow and easy. Feel a lightness filling your head. The lightness indicates clarity.

Now become aware of your partner's size, shape, and temperature. Begin to feel the energy flow as you are becoming more connected with that person, feeling less threatened. Really get into it. Concentrate on the energy flow between you. Become one with it. The less resistance, the less threat, the less fear, the greater the flow. Let it flow. There is nothing to be afraid of.

Now try to get in touch with the pull of the flow of energy coming up from the earth, the same magnetic force that creates the gravitational effect. Open the bottoms of your feet as if they are vents, and allow the earth's magnetism to enter into you. Allow the flow of this energy to move upward into you. Feel the weight of its magnetism. Don't restrict it.

Tap into that flow. See it, imagine it, feel it as a flow melting through you, flowing up through you like lava. Feel it flowing freely into your muscles, your bones, your nerves. The vents in your feet will slowly and gently open up wider and wider. Feel the weight of the earth's magnetism, the raw power of it. Let it flow up through your ankles, your lower legs. It might feel uncomfortable at first; bear with it—it will break through finally. Feel it moving up through your knees, going up into your thighs, your hips, settling in your belly or lower back. Now feel it flow up through your chest and upper back and shoulders. It's a flow. It's magnetic.

Let it flow through your arms and elbows. Let it flow through your forearms, your wrists, your fingers, your hands. Let it break through little energetic logjams (nothing can stop it) and finally into your partner's fingers. Now that the flow is started, notice your breathing—how slow, how gentle it is. Slowly open your eyes.

This is a very exciting and useful exercise. It is helpful for eliminating various bone, liver, and skull ailments. You'll find it different every time you use it, especially if you do it with someone you have never seen before. It will also vary when you do it with a new person each time. Each one will find it helpful according to their own needs.

Over the years, I have used this exercise in my intensive seminars on Spiritual Healing, and people have reported many types of responses in what they sensed or felt as well as in healing results. Here are samples of the more frequently related responses:

Susie: "I was totally relaxed. I could feel the flow circulate through us."

Judy: "I felt so calm. My headache totally dissipated."

Gina: "My head was just throbbing. As you were talking about our feet opening up as vents, I felt myself wanting to cry because I felt I had to trust my partner, and then I opened myself up to trusting people, which is so new for me."

Art: "I felt a vibration in our palms; it was really warm, and I could feel a rhythm."

Kathy: "My leg muscles were really shaking, and I'm very, very hot right now."

Jill: "All of a sudden, I felt like I was very heavy, leaning to the left. I felt we were both leaning and I was going to fall over." (That was actually the magnetic force throwing both of them into balance, where they had been out of balance.)

8

Getting Ready to Heal

No darkness, no shadow
Can stand in the light.

I. The Focus of Healing

I work under the assumption that we are all healers. Each of us has the ability to listen to that Voice within each of us. That Voice is an idea, a revelation. It is clear. It has the intelligence to know what to do, as long as our point of reference is giving, perceptive, and receptive.

If we decide to work with other people, our place is to listen purposefully. In healing, we can place our hands near or on someone. While we do this, we are allowing the Voice and its clarity to take over, which occurs automatically when we intend it to happen. The Voice takes over without judgment or condemnation. Without our interference, it knows what needs to be done, what needs to happen, and what does not need to happen.

While working with someone, if we find ourselves with a judgment of what we want to change in the other person, we sabotage our desire to help. The trick is to allow the healing to happen without getting in the way. As the expression goes, "Let go and let God." After all, we do not heal; Self does; the Creator does. We are simply vehicles that allow it to express itself through us. We must constantly remind ourselves of that and understand that the process is no longer under our control; otherwise, we are playing God and not letting God be God. Then the healing will happen only partially, for a short while, or not at all.

II. How to Focus Your Thinking for Healing

The embryonic fluid state, which I associate with the Universal Mind, carries all the possibilities of what can be. It carries an electromagnetic charge as well. We have the ability to willfully collect this charge and utilize it. We can then control its effects. Some people call this charge Spirit; some call it by other names.

This intangible force is at work at all times within you. I use it as a basis for working with someone's field in healing. I experience the electromagnetic charge, the emanations from the other person's field, flowing into my field and extending beyond, intermeshing endlessly with other fields. I automatically tune into and perceive all the fields as a single field of information, enabling me to retrieve information from the flow of events in which this person has participated. Any issue, situation, or problem that they have can be traced to its causal moment within that composite of events. By holding an image of the person in their perfected state—the opposite of what they are projecting—the causal moment that has kept them from realizing their perfected state generally becomes apparent, consciously or subconsciously, and begins to dissipate.

VISUALIZE THE PERSON IN PERFECTION

Focus on the person in front of you. Imagine this person in what you perceive to be a perfect form. See the body to be harmonious, whole and perfect, working as a finely tuned machine in perfect flow. You are using your imagination— imaging in action. You are watching this perfectly tuned person fully functioning, and you are holding that thought in your mind the best you can, for as long as you can, without letting any extraneous thoughts come in.

Even if the person is complaining of some disease, it isn't necessary to accept it as a conversation of which you have to be a part. See only the perfection, because that is what you are working with. If for some reason you are unable to hold this visual image, you must begin again. If you can't hold the image of perfection the second time, remember, you can start over a thousand times. God doesn't care and will not tell you that you are bad.

Once you have concentrated on that image, let God take it and let go. This initial step may take a minute or more, although it can occur in seconds once you have become more adept with this process.

After you have visualized everything in perfection, give attention to what might appear to be the physical or emotional disorder. If you are working on a specific organ or limb, focus on that.

So first, you're tuning into the concept of a perfect, well-operating physical shell, consisting of every cellular piece that brings the body together in an electrical matrix. You are concentrating and seeing the perfection.

The next step is seeing this perfection working without the physical discomfort. Again, healing is a universal principle, a law, which takes the impressions of our thoughts and acts upon them.

Let's say the person you are healing says, "I'm sick. I don't feel well. I need attention. I need a drink of booze. I have to stay home from school." These complaints are forms of self-sabotage. Once you have focused on the person's thought with an image of wholeness and perfection, your thought will bind to the other person.

It is very important for the other person to also want to change.

The other person will find themselves thinking along the same lines as long as you are thinking, and knowing, perfect wholeness with surety. If you can maintain that thought with the fire of desire within you, the Creator, your Source, God, will take over from that point.

Your thought can be used to eliminate another person's destructive thought pattern (or in self healing, your own destructive pattern). Don't worry; if you do, worry will be your intent and prayer, which will sabotage your intention of wholeness. Worry is a form of resistance.

Healing only works through trust and knowing in Self, God, Jesus, the Nameless One, Universal Mind—whatever name you choose. When I first started working with healing, I would put my hands over someone's head and tell God to get busy, because I wasn't sure what I was doing. And God did get busy and took over, because I trusted that it would happen. I knew it wasn't me.

KNOW THAT IT IS DONE

Finish the session with your realization and trust that it is done. Walk away; don't let another thought come in your head. If it does, you have sabotaged the effort. If this is the case, start over. It is not bad or wrong to start over.

That's why it is so important to learn the practice of focus by maintaining concentrated effort. Concentration and meditation are useful tools to help us learn focus, intent, and the presence of something greater than ourselves.

Again, the law and the truth are the basis of healing. A person does not heal; the law and the truth do. We don't treat each organ of the body as a separate part, but we see the body to be as whole and perfect as a finely tuned machine. When you feel the healing sensations, you are experiencing the law in action.

The law knows nothing about disease; it only acts. I've seen tumors disappear; I've seen thousands of people's lives change drastically and dramatically. All of these so-called miracles happen because we have allowed something greater to move through us. If that is true, we are not doing anything except serving as vehicles. We had no idea how something was going to turn out or what was going to transpire in the other person (or even in ourselves). But our Source knew what to do in a perfect way.

When I was starting out healing and felt unsure of what I was doing, I would say, "OK, God, this person has a cold." Then I would envision that person in a perfect, clear-headed state of mind and body, without a cold. I imagined the cold melting away and the person in a joyful frame of mind. Initially the act would me take a couple of minutes (although with practice it can take just moments). And it would be so. The person that had the cold would feel better either immediately or the next day upon awakening. (Remember, though, having a cold is OK; it's a cleansing that the body is going through. It is a process that the body uses to eliminate toxins. But I see it this way: why do we need to suffer?)

In any case, I would imagine the cold melting away and the person in a joyful frame of mind. Once you see this image completely, drop it like a hot potato and let go of the impression, because if you have any thought of sabotage or negation, you will have to begin again.

That's how I started working many years ago, and as time went on, the process began to flow easily. You can start this way too. It is a great place to start. You can learn to focus completely for just that moment. Practice this, and it will develop within you.

You can create anything with your thoughts. By my understanding, there are very few incurable diseases if the individuals you are working with will accept what you are doing and know it is meant to be for them. Your work with them will help them immediately or over time. The effects also depend upon the influence of the atmosphere immediately around the person, including relatives or friends, medical personnel, what they've read in articles, or how they have been influenced by television.

Perhaps the disease was supposed to be part of the individual's life, because that is what their whole life has brought them to. But you can help them ease or eliminate the symptoms or be more comfortable within the remaining time of their life. Healing may not necessarily work the way we want or thought, but through understanding and trust, something more is happening for them and for us, by something that isn't us.

As we build the image of the person in perfection, we are planting seeds of what the person has already known but needs to be reminded of. This helps to bring back the memories from the Self of what we have forgotten—remembering it all together, bringing it all back together, to what we were originally born to be in the first place. Until now, we've taken ourselves down the difficult road of life, following the survival mode approach, because that is what we have been taught for generations. It has become hereditary and is in our genetic code. But once you have started to master this practice, you learn that you truly have the power of life and death over creation. You will see this manifest not only in yourself but in other people as well. You will become more adept in other aspects of creation, both nonlinear and physical. That's how dynamic the art of healing can be.

III. Morphic Fields and Auras

We all have morphic fields, the intangible transmitters and receivers of information within and about our being. Morphic fields, sometimes called auras, carry memories of information regarding all of individuals' past memories and responses. These fields also carry information about our current state of being at any given moment. They are connected to the physical body and can be found both within and around the body. Everything about our existence is found in our morphic fields.

There are a number of ways to experience morphic fields. You can see an emanation of light around a person or object. This light reflects the frequency, vibratory rate, and the life consciousness that the being or object carries. As you develop the ability to see this light, you will be able to see that certain objects have different vibratory rates. This sight develops with the experience of *gazing*. Gazing is an art in itself and can be developed by anyone who wishes to see another aspect of reality.

Many people are able to see or sense clear light or colors around others. This is an indicator of a greater consciousness that allows us to work with healing. When a trauma is released through healing, it can sometimes be seen as waves coming off a person's body, much like heat waves off a highway on a hot day. Some people see the release as smoke, some smell it, and others see it as wisps coming off the body. Sometimes people see the healing through a person's tears. It is easier to see this energy with peripheral vision.

The method I'll explain to you is really quite easy. Practice gazing about six inches above someone's head and beyond, and then let your peripheral vision take over. Practice this, and it will become automatic. You can also accomplish this effect by staring at someone's forehead, tuning into your peripheral vision, and letting it wander into the space beyond the body.

Some people see colors around other people's heads. If you see a reddish or pinkish glow, this indicates a headache. If you see gray, stick with it until it takes form as a color or a specific visual form of some other nature. If you see globules following someone, this indicates they are thinking very intently about quandaries in their life. If you see a pink glow away from the head, the headache happened several days ago. The farther away from the body, the greater length of time has passed since the injury or trauma. The more you practice this, the more your visuals will have meaning.

Not everyone sees colors. Each of us has our own unique way of perceiving. By practicing, you will learn about your own unique ability.

IV. The Disease Body

The morphic field may show you the disease body. The disease body is the biological and physical manifestation of dis-ease, and is carried in the memory of learned drama and trauma. It is basically composed of ammonia and methane gas, which have a deteriorating and decomposing effect. This is the disturbance you can feel, see, or smell on the person you are working with. It's a cellular combustion process whose effects you are witnessing, possibly both before and after physical manifestation.

This gaseous body often looks grayish in color, or a distorted, dingy yellow. It could be other colors, but they will seem very dingy and muddy looking. You can sometimes feel it as a pressure, a weight, an electrical discharge, or tingling, which is the consciousness of light deteriorating the disease. It will sometimes feel like a void, or it will feel dirty or sticky. Use the surface of the skin on your palms to feel it.

Some people can smell disease. Each disease has its own odor. Arthritis smells like burning rubber. Cancer has a very sickly sweet smell, like burning sugar.

Each person perceives disease uniquely. As you practice with touch and nontouch healing (including healing with thought), you will become more familiar with the different ways you experience other people's disease bodies.

For everything you feel, see, or smell that is skewed or out of sync in a morphic field, there is a directly related symptom in that person, physically, biologically, emotionally, or mentally. Every dysfunctional dynamic that someone does not attend to will eventually manifest on a biological and physical level to varying degrees. Emotional distress will certainly develop into physical and biological distress, which you can feel in a person's field. When feeling someone's field, therefore, you are feeling their *current* state of being: their emotional state of being in the moment, their history, and the life that will be.

As you work with someone, don't be concerned about catching someone else's distress. Remember, it's only energy. You are only feeling the cellular memory from distress experienced during a person's life. *You are not getting their cooties.* You can't. Another simple truth is this: *no darkness, no shadow can stand in the light.*

Many years ago, during a healing circle in Des Plaines, Illinois, people would ask me questions about getting sick from others. In my arrogant, show-off way, sometimes in front of a couple of hundred people, I would put my hands on someone and pull out their disease or consciousness of injury. Then in front of all these people, I would bring the disease or injury consciousness into my own body. They would always ooh and ahh, and I would laugh. Then I would tell them, "Why be shocked? It's only energy!" We can be sick from someone else's stuff because that is what we have learned to be, or we can utilize this destructive energetic for life. We have the ability to transform destructive understanding into constructive understanding.

TRUSTING WHAT YOU SENSE IN OTHERS

When you begin healing, you usually start by learning to feel the disease body. This sense provides some proof that people need to know that there might be more to life than we were aware of. Then you have to trust what you are imagining: accept what you perceive to be true. Once you trust yourself when you are standing before someone and utilizing the energies of vibration and frequency, you will more and more clearly see your ability to heal. Once you have been practicing with feeling the disease body, you will become more acutely tuned to the different feelings of each and every disease. You will see that these images may occur for just a flash of a second, and you will learn to tune in. You will learn what to watch for.

Asthma is usually a form of panic disorder usually resulting from a traumatic birthing experience or some other experience, usually from between the ages of two and eleven years. It is a pattern that has taken on a physical manifestation. To find out when it started, listen to your intuition, and let it plant a seed concerning the origin of this disorder (either within the person you are working with, or within yourself). Wait until you feel something happen in the person's body. Concentrate on looking past them, and you will somehow sense when it all began based on your own way of perceiving. Tell them what you are perceiving; they will find this information useful, either immediately or later. In some way according to their needs, it will shift them out of the trauma from the earlier causal moment that led to a reaction of asthma.

With people with arthritis, there is stiffness and an inability to grasp an idea or concept in their life—an inability to grasp issues because of a stubborn understanding. This happens on an emotional level as well. As you work with someone with arthritis, you may sense a rigidity in thinking or a die-hard attitude. You may notice them stiffening up their hands as they speak, or they may feel their stomach or neck tightening up. You can pose questions to determine if they have ways of being rigid that may be limiting the expression of their wholeness.

Your questions and suggestions can be subtle or direct, depending on what intuitive direction you get. But once the rigid patterns are out in the open, there is no more reason to hide them, and they have the freedom to express themselves more flexibly. Trust that what you offer will serve for healing.

V. Using Scanning for Healing

Scanning is the process used to tune in to someone's morphic field and work with their areas of disturbance and distortion. The following exercise will introduce you to the experience of sensing another person's energy when you are scanning.

THE PALM-TO-PALM EXERCISE:
SENSING ANOTHER'S ENERGY

Make sure you are in a quiet environment so you can focus more easily. Stand up and face your partner. Place your hands in the pat-a-cake position. Bend your elbows at a ninety-degree angle, and turn your hands so one of your palms is facing the ceiling, the other facing the floor. Put the left palm up and the right palm down. Have your partner do the same.

Now place your palms facing each other's. Your palms should not be touching. Hold your palms one to one and a half inches away from your partner. Do not make physical contact.

Close your eyes. Begin to feel the energy between your hands and theirs. Feel it on your palms. This energy within each of you is waiting and begging to be given out. It is the life force that is flowing between the two of you—the flow of life's energy. Slowly start to move your hands up and down a little bit. Feel the sensation on the surface of the skin of your hands. Move slowly.

Continue to move your hands slowly up and down a little. You will feel something between your hands. It will feel like a pressure inside the space between your hands. Feel the attraction and the pull of the energy. Experience the inner and outer limits of the electrical matrix of your bodies by slightly pulling your hands away. Feel how far the energy extends and how tall it is. Feel its intensity. Move your hands apart until you barely feel it, and open your eyes to see how far apart your hands are.

While you are doing this exercise, if you feel something in a special place in your body (for example, your wrist), that is because you are freeing an emotional and/or physiological trauma there. This sensation is what I refer to as a slight "logjam." The flow of energy, life force, is clearing the logjam in each area.

HOW TO SCAN

Become focused. Tune in to Self and feel the part of your being that is extruding outside of your body. Your eyes can be open or closed. God doesn't care. Go with whichever way you are more comfortable with.

Now with your partner standing in front of you, position your hands over the top of their head without touching them. There is no need for direct contact. Wait until you feel that same sensory body that you felt with the palm-to-palm exercise. Your partner may also feel something in the head or above it, or may not feel anything. If the latter is the case, this doesn't make them wrong or bad; nor does it mean that nothing is happening.

Usually I tell my students, "Some feel things because they need to in their journey, or else they wouldn't trust. Others don't always feel these things because they just don't need to feel anything in their journey. Or maybe they already have learned trust, or maybe they perceive in another way."

Stay focused. Move your hands around a little, keeping them side by side or slightly splitting them apart by a few inches. See which technique works best for you to continue sensing your partner's energy.

With your hands, travel slowly down the body, along the neck, the shoulders, each arm, and working your way down to the waist area. Move slowly. At some place, you will feel a little distortion in the field that the other person's body is emanating. It could feel like a void or a sensation of a different kind, such as heat, cold, or static.

While scanning, try to get an inner sense of what feels odd in those spots of distortion. Be sensitive to yourself. Let your Self tell you what might not be correct in this person's life. Pay attention to energy and dynamic changes. Concentrate and use your focused intent to sense, see, feel, or hear an impression. You might get perceptions of pressure, heat, cold, emptiness, or even static. That's exciting!

Ask the person if the impression you have might be associated with their disease, injury, or dilemma in any way. (In the next section, we'll be discussing the time lines that will enable you to identify these sensations.) Let them discover what they can extract from what you have told them. Then wait until that feeling of distortion goes away. This sensation may feel like a flow or a sense of clarity. Tune into your unique perception of what you are knowing in the moment. Have your partner tune into their perception as well.

Tell each other what you feel and when you feel it. Tell each other when you notice some kind of change that might be happening, not only in the immediate area you're working with, but in other parts of the body that might be affected as well. You or your partner will feel a flow. In its healthiest form, the flow of the body's life force or heat cycle is felt at approximately sixteen pulses per minute. If you notice a variation in that rhythm, keep your attention there until the pulsing breaks free of its distortion and resumes a healthy flow. Then you'll also notice that if, say, the pulses were only about twelve beats per minute, they'll now be about sixteen beats.

Wait until the pulsing (or whatever you feel) dissipates, goes away, or flows. Then go to the next area where you might sense logjams. Keep moving down the body until you get to the waist. Then wait there. You have to move slowly.

If you get some flash of information, whether you hear it, see it, or feel it, do not negate this; accept it. Trust this. Do not edit or try to change in mind what you perceive; speak it out plainly and honestly. Ask your partner if there's a memory of something similar regarding this area. Something happened in this life that is being reflected in every area where you feel a distortion or difference. At one time, this person had an injury or an ache or pain or an emotional drama or trauma there. They are carrying a memory of it in the cells and tissue as a result of shock. It could have been a long time ago. What is being perceived here now is applicable for this moment. They are still identifying with it in their life and they are still reliving in the memory.

BE SENSITIVE TO ANY CHANGES

Be sensitive to any temperature changes, open spaces, or other sensations in particular spots as you scan them. For example, anxiety or worry is generally located around the shoulders and neck, sometimes in the head and/or gut. Every person carries it in a unique way.

When you feel something farther away from the body, it is more identifiable as being from the past. This is the drama and trauma of something that happened a long time ago but is still affecting the individual. You can still work at this spot. They may or may not feel or associate with anything they recognize from that past experience as you work, but what you are doing will help to change the current effects of that causal time period.

Even if you take your hands down when you are working with a person, when you raise them again you could still feel where you left off. However, you may find that some part of what you were experiencing has dissipated.

WAIT UNTIL YOU FEEL THE FLOW

Once you sense some type of distortion, stay with it until you feel the flow, as subtle or dramatic as it may be. You'll be able to notice the flow in your hands, in your arms, or both. When you feel this happening, the person is becoming more healed. You are helping to initiate true regeneration at a molecular level—in this case, with the "spiritual molecule." I believe that for any physical thing, there is also a spiritual counterpart. You are actually giving life from a different perspective: you are helping the molecule to remember, to remind itself of its perfection. (Always keep in mind that Self, God, Creator is doing the actual healing.) You will feel your indicators. It might be difficult to perceive them, but they will come in practice and awareness. You don't have to provide anything of your own except intent. That's why focus is important. The more intensely you can go in wanting to understand and perceive, the greater effect you will create within the other person's body.

You started doing this not knowing what you would be doing or feeling. Though you'll become familiar with general indicators, intent takes over, with its own consciousness and intelligence. That consciousness knows what to do with or without us. We're just there as vehicles.

The person being scanned may need to interact with you again in the future, or this one experience may be enough to plant a seed that the person can take and work with from there. You will know, and you will be able to make that judgment call after the session.

VI. Scanning and Time Lines

When you are finished working on the upper body, then begin on the lower body, working in the same way. You will start at the waist and move down. Once you reach the hips, begin to work with one leg at a time.

There are age associations with various segments of the lower body. If you feel a void or a change in an adult's field while your hands are near a certain area, it corresponds to experiences at a certain age relevant to that area:

The top of the waist relates to age twenty-one or near it.

The center of the hip bone relates to age seventeen.

The kneecap relates to age seven.

The ankle relates to age one.

The foot relates to the first year of life.

In my seminars, I teach how to perceive and use these age associations in much more detail. They have mental, emotional, and physical aspects, as well as differences between males and females. But even with the brief description provided here, you can begin to pay attention to these parts of the body and their age associations as you are scanning. When you feel distortion in between these areas (for example, the area between the hip, at the bottom of the buttock cheek, and the top of the waist would correspond to the ages of fourteen to twenty-one), you can focus on that age range and get information about what happened and at what age. With practice, you will sense things much more quickly and accurately. This topic merits a book of its own.

VII. Healing Happens as You Scan

Accept the healing as done; don't doubt it. Doubt will only serve to sabotage your intent. Healing will only happen when you and your doubts get out of the way. All you have to do is trust, and it is done. Do not look over your shoulder and second-guess what happened.

CONCENTRATED FOCUS

Scanning is a combination of intention and concentrated focus. Concentrated focus is critical to reaching your goal. The intense ability to focus and sustain that focus is the basis of other-dimensional mindfulness. It enables us to control the power of life and death, of recreation.

Many years ago, I was fortunate to be able to watch a woman work with a child. The child arrived with a broken arm. This woman held the little broken arm on her lap. She was working with what she described as magnetic forces. Within several minutes, the broken bone actually moved from the broken area to the natural position. This woman used electromagnetic healing, a very strong and powerful tool. This is an example of what can happen with the use of concentrated focus, intention, and magnetic forces.

In a similar way, some people are known for mind-over-matter spoon-bending demonstrations. They work with the electromagnetic composition, heat, friction, and vibration of the materials to quicken the vibration of the molecular structure and bend the spoon. They too work with focused concentration and intention.

HEALING WITH SCANNING

A man came to see me who had been diagnosed with a nerve disease that left him in extreme pain. The nerves were in a constant state of deterioration, and he could no longer walk because of the intense pain on the bottom of his feet and calf muscles. He was diagnosed when he was ten years old and was told there was no cure. He came to me as a forty-year-old wearing special braces for his legs, which helped ease the discomfort. The pain in his calf muscles was not as intense as it had been since he had the braces made, since they gave him good physical support.

I worked on him in a focused way, through scanning, to see how I could help. In the scanning process, I was able to get into specific areas of his legs and feet that related to the various ages of his life. The next day, he called me and was practically yelling on the phone, "You're not going to believe this! My calf muscle is bigger, and I don't need the braces anymore! My feet don't hurt anymore!" This pain originated for him around thirty years prior to my visit with him. It had been growing since then and made him who he was until that day.

Healing helps these causal memories to melt away, changing someone's life. This has been validated for me thousands of times during healing sessions. I am awed by the gift that all of us have to offer ourselves and one another, if we can simply tune in and understand that it is available to each and every one of us.

WE DO NOT CONTROL THE OUTCOME

It is important to understand that people are affected by healing each in their own way, always within the parameters of their own speed, in their time, in the course of what is to be in their life. It is not up to us to decide just how a person is affected by our healing. We do not know, and the outcome is not for us to determine. There are so many facets of a person's life that are affected from even one causal moment that we do not know how things will progress. Our only resort is to trust.

It is also important to know that healing does not, and cannot, harm another. You can do only good with healing. Trust this and know this; after all, we are not the ones doing the healing.

VIII. Frequently Asked Questions

Q: What if you want to work on someone who does not believe in healing? They think it is all bunk, hocus-pocus nonsense. Can they still gain the effects of healing?
A: It is not wrong to do good. You can provide the benefits of healing to anyone as long as it is your intent to do such a thing. I know many people who have helped others who were asleep at the time.

Nonetheless, I won't have anyone challenging me. At a large gathering, someone came up to me and listened as several others and I were having a conversation. At a moment of pause in the conversation, this fellow bellowed, "I hear that you're a healer. My leg hurts. Heal it." It was a very awkward moment, and I felt that he was just challenging me and that his leg really didn't hurt. With everyone around watching what my reaction would be, I looked at him and said, "Make an appointment." Even if his situation was real, I saw that he was still putting full weight on his knee, and I had noticed that he had walked up to us without grimacing. If the situation was real, I would have immediately taken him aside to work with him. Why someone does this kind of thing, I don't know. We'll always be presented with challenges. It's in the mass mind to present challenges in our path.

Your intent is the key to helping others. Remember, though, you do not decide what needs to be healed; the Creator does. It's not the god out there on the third cloud up and two to the left; it's the Divinity and Self within. You must trust this.

Q: What if I ask a person if I can heal them, and they say no?
A: It is not important to get someone's permission to help them. I have worked with many people without their knowing it, nor will I ever mention anything to them or others. You do not need permission from people to help them do better and feel better. If you think you need someone's permission to pray for them, it was something you read or learned from someone else's inadequacy. After all, with every person we think of or meet or converse with, there is always prayer involved anyway—every day!

If someone refuses healing, it may be because they are not well enough to make their own decisions in the first place; perhaps that is the very predicament that brought them to this consequence. Many people don't know that they can ask for prayers or intercessions for healing. I don't feel that I ever have to tell them that I worked with them. In some situations, if I do insist to myself that if I have to tell them what I did, either before or afterward, then I really have to take a look at my motive. It would definitely be a signal of wanting to heal for my own edification and glorification.

Q: But what if it's not the right thing or the right time for them to be healed?

A: We can still work with them because we are leaving it up to the inner Self, the Nameless One within, that determines how and what healing will happen. I won't force myself on anyone. If they are absolute in their no, it's just not for me to intrude in their life. I'll walk away. It's still up to me if I feel compelled to say prayers for them, though I usually drop it not thinking again of the person again. I personally will not work with someone who doesn't want me to work on them or was forced by another to be in front of me. Nor will I work with anyone who just wants to test me. When someone approaches us, it must be for help, and from their need, from their heart. When a couple of people have come for their appointments, while greeting them at the door, I have told them to leave. Maybe it is not our place to be their healer. We never know. Nor does it matter what we know or think if we are truly serving humanity.

I also understand that every once in a while, I may not be the correct one to heal a particular person. Maybe flower remedies or medical intervention are better for them. But I do know that there is some possible intervention for everyone, with our unique minds, bodies, and experiences.

Q: Do you feel energy moving through you all the time that you are working on someone?

A: I do most often feel the energies moving in the Creator, though please understand that it isn't necessary to feel it.

As I look back over the years, I see some times when I felt there was no movement of life force, and the people had also told me they hadn't felt or experienced anything. But days, weeks, or even years later, some of them approached me to say that they felt better or were healed. Those that do feel the energetic response need to, and those that don't feel the response don't necessarily need to. The person I'm working on does not always feel what I feel.

At times we'll perceive that an emotional catharsis is coming on in someone, or that there is a constriction, a holding back in emotional release. This cathartic moment can break or release that constriction. We can sense and feel the vibrational pattern of stuckness: it's similar to the pressure of a soap bubble. It's not so stuck that the person is dying, but something is not totally flowing. I usually refer to these as logjams. That's the way I feel them. I'll rest my hands on the inflicted area until the bubble breaks. I know it is done when I feel the flow through my hands or arm or body. That is one of my indicators. You may have a similar or different indicator.

There have been times when I do not know precisely what I am sensing at first. I have to wait for the information, though my impressions are mostly immediate.

Q: Most of the time when I am healing, the people feel the warmth. Can you elaborate on that?
A: That was simply some people's experience; don't get stuck in that belief. One person I was treating said that they were feeling very cold. Then their body began shivering and shaking violently and uncontrollably right in front of me. It made me nervous, but as uncertain as I was, I main-

tained my demeanor and let the process continue until the situation broke. Then the person was fine. Some will feel the heat or cold; others will feel static or more powerful currents; still others may feel a sensation of air moving through them.

Q: Can you explain what healing has to do with being an empath?
A: There is no reason for you to ever take on someone else's personal experience of drama or trauma, emotionally or physically. It's not your experience, and never was. It is their experience.

Q: Can we get spirit guides to help us or do healing for us? There are times when I call them in to finish my work.
A: Your question suggests that you are feeling insecure about trusting yourself. This lack of surety changes as we work with healing and gain experience .

It was a giveaway to say that you were one doing the healing. When something began to happen, you got nervous and declared inside that someone outside of you did the healing. This way, if you don't see the results you want, you can blame the failure on someone else! We all do that at times: we renege on our responsibility and fall into denial (although this is a stronger pattern for some than for others). Now is your opportunity to look at this pattern.

As soon as you start thinking, "I'm nervous that they may not get a fuller reaction or may not get any at all; I hope that God is doing something," that is your sabotage, because you are pulling back a little bit. Even so, the other is still being helped to varying degrees according to their needs and yours. As soon as you consciously recognize a nervousness within you, say, "OK, boss, I am not quite sure what is happening or what to do here. You take over here." And let it take over!

Q: Can you work on children when they are sleeping?
A: Yes. We can put our hands above them without touching, scan their entire body, and wait until we feel a flow of life force with our hands. When we can get to approximately sixteen pulsations a minute, we know the body is in flow and the situation is taken care of.

If the child has a fever, you might place your right hand slightly touching their head and the left hand slightly touching the lower abdominal area. Observe the color of fever, which is some hue of red. Observe the red slowly turning to a luminescent orange color which completely replaces the red. Keep your hands in that position until you feel a subtle or dramatic flow or breeze or gentle current of air move evenly and consistently between your hands. The way to succeed in this is to maintain your focus until the process is complete. There are also other ways to dissipate a fever, but this one often helps.

Q: How do you help someone who has chronic pain or discomfort? What do you mean when you say you can help them embrace the pain?
A: A chronic sufferer might be creating the pain to fulfill some aspect of his or her emotional development, but people can get beyond this pain to a place where they no longer need to suffer. When you are embracing the pain, you are stepping into it as an interested observer, with curiosity, without par-

ticipating in it. Because you are not fighting it, not suppressing it anymore, it no longer interferes in your life cycle.

Another way of embracing the pain is by recognizing possible causal times in your life when it was the worst or when it subsided. Someone might also want to ask their Self what happened emotionally at those times. Was the pressure off in that moment? Was there a reprieve in the momentary dynamic of self-dissatisfaction? How did you feel emotionally right before the pain subsided?

Initially work with your hands to find the areas of discontent in the body. Most discontents relate to the stomach, heart, and head areas. Rely on your intuitive abilities to scan the person for the area(s) of source. Objectively step into the pain and find the source. Remember, there is never a reason to take anything on from another.

Another way to work with someone's pain using the above technique is to go even deeper into the discomfort without resistance and try to find peace with it. This sounds foolish to many, but it will most often make the discomfort subside or disappear.

Q: Will we feel the same sense of healing with every person?
A: It's not going to be the same with every person or situation. For example, sometimes you may come to a logjam. Nothing is ever completely blocked, or there would be no life; there is always some lifeforce flowing. I like using the term *logjam* because when a beaver builds a dam, there is still some water that flows through. If that weren't the case with, say, our arm, it would shrivel up and eventually fall off. Unless death is imminent, there will always be a trickle or stream of life force. If we can stay there for a moment

or longer until we feel the flow, then the life force will open up the flow to some degree. Then we move on and can later return to reinforce what we have done.

The logjam often represents various dramas and traumas that affect us emotionally and physiologically. By providing a reminder to the life force and giving it a chance to break through, we are working with the immediate situation; on some occasions, we may very well be saving a person's life.

Q: I don't think I have proved to myself that I can do this. I still have this question about whether what I see around people is accurate and what I feel is really more than just sensations in my hands.

A: You may need to repeat your experiences again and again. You will doubt those too. You may do this again and again, doubting it every time. That doubt is the mass mind in action, telling you this can't be happening: it is not logical in terms of what you have been taught. This is our immediate intellectual and conditioned response. That's what we've been conditioned to do. Believe me, I have been in your place. You may need to build your proof just a little bit at a time. Once you see an effect, a difference, either immediately or within twenty-four hours, you will accept a little bit more. Try again. Keep at it. Over time, you will see for yourself that this is part of reality.

You are smart to doubt what you are doing. I challenge you to keep doubting. I must do that too; sometimes I have learned through experience, and I am still learning through doubt. But I wouldn't have learned what I know now unless I had the experience before.

Another way to prove that this is real is, when people come to you, tell them not to tell you what their situations of discomfort are. Then scan them in the ways described above. As you find areas of energetic logjams, let them verify or deny them. Even initially, most often they will verify.

Q: When my partner worked on me, I had my eyes closed. I felt heat in the cavities of my face when his hands were near my face. When I opened my eyes, he was working in another area, but I still felt the heat in my face. Why?
A: This is because the healing was still working. It's what I call "fire fighting fire." A greater consciousness is left inside somewhere in the body to do the work. We don't need to do anything. We are letting it take over from there. Your partner was also working on your abdominal area; the abdomen always relates to the head and vice versa. Also, as we have intent in helping another, even if we are working on one part of the body, another part may be affected. The greater mind always knows what to do if our heart has intent.

Q: I came to see you about six weeks ago for help with eating lots of fatty things, and you worked on this for me. Ever since then, I've noticed a part of my brain that still sees something fatty and says, "Oh, yes, eat that." Then I'll take a bite or two, get nauseous, and put it down. It's been great. I can drive by Colonel Sanders now so easily.
A: Hooray! That is because I was able to work with the causal moment that created this craving in you and break the muscle of its energy. You must have been ready to let it go; I just provided the catalyst. But the mind of the world

will always try to grab you back. That mind doesn't want you to succeed, and it will be there for the rest of your life. But you'll also see that over time, those moments of temptation will diminish. It's as though those initial thoughts lose their life by not being utilized.

Q: Is psychological disease the same as physiological? Does it feel the same?

A: Yes. It's of a similar nature and composition. They work in tandem with each other; it doesn't matter which comes first. I feel them the same way, but I work with them in a different way. (I go into this understanding a lot more in my intuitional seminars.) To put it simply, I don't feel the psychological; more often I see it and hear in the person's first words—*if* it's my place to work with it.

Q: Can you clarify the various stages that take someone from a causal moment up to the state where physical and biological disease occurs?

A: First and hypothetically, say that at the age of nine, someone gave you a knuckle sandwich in the shoulder. That is a shock trauma. If it was in front of others, it was probably embarrassing. From that moment onward, that scenario has been stored in you. Later in life, maybe decades later, we find ourselves with discomforts, arthritis, or another distress that is emotionally disrupting our life. That original hit to the shoulder remained as a bruise in that area. There's a lot more to say about that, but I wanted to keep the answer simple.

Another answer: a mental perception regarding a thought or event generally stems from the causal moment or moments when we first experienced the event, as well as mass mind conversations we've been taught all our lives. This original thought becomes our living prayer, because it is what we have learned and therefore what we are taught to attract. From that moment on, it will manifest itself in one direction of thought or another. In other words, what we feel and what we think is what we teach our children to be. They will resemble us in both patterns and ideas.

Next comes the enactment of the emotional response—the hurt, the fear, the pain, the anxiety, the sadness, the distress. We may even be responding to someone else's experience. You can empathize with these feelings because they are of your past too. When you feel hurt, despair, sadness, pain, or anxiety for yourself or someone else, you have planted a seed inside yourself. This is the causal moment that shifts your life into a potentially destructive manifestation.

After the emotional onset comes the biological manifestation. This can happen right away or can be manifested later in the form of an illness.

Once you recognize this causal moment within yourself, you will realize you no longer have to be chained to the past anymore. You can let go of it. You are not there anymore.

Q: How can I get rid of my own headache?
A: Sometimes we need to rest, and the headache will dissipate. Sometimes a headache is due to digestive situations. And sometimes the following exercises will help:

If you have a headache or you feel one coming on, try the following: When you hear yourself think or even say out loud, "Oh no, I feel this headache coming on," or "Darn,

I hope this isn't going to be one of those headaches," at that moment you can catch yourself in your thought and say, "Wait. If I can realize that the headache is coming on, I can also realize and imagine something else. I'm going to do something here. I'm going to step out of myself and see the headache as a stream and let it go right on by me. I'm going to stop and think that when I step back, I will not let the stream hit me." You will realize that you didn't have a headache for that moment or two. Now try it again. Step back again. Again, for a moment you didn't have that headache.

Now we can take this one step further and say to the headache, "OK, I see you. I feel you. I sense you. But you are going to have to wait a moment; I have something else to do. Wait here, and I will be right back." Then ditch it. Walk away quickly; think of something else to get your mind off of it. Watch what happens: it will probably be lessened, you'll forget that you had a headache, and you will not have it any longer. You will soon realize that you can set a pattern where you never again have to take on that headache. You can practice this exercise with many other discomforts as well.

We have the power of life and death over creation. If we just practice it, it becomes real just as easily as the drama and trauma have become real. These are all tools for us. As a matter of fact, you can get to the point where it is more difficult to get out of sync with your body and thinking patterns than to stay in sync. It also becomes more obvious when we are beginning to get out of sync. Then we know what to do to help ourselves.

Q: If you feel someone else's pain, it becomes your own prayer. How can you reverse that? I can't imagine seeing someone in pain without feeling sorry for them in some way. I thought empathy is good. Isn't it?

A: Learning compassion is good and desirable, but here is a little more about empathy. This is where we have to step out of ourselves and let go and let God. Say, "OK, God, you are using me to work on this person. I don't want to take any of this stuff on. I don't want to leave here with whatever they have. So you go ahead and take care of it."

Accept that something else is happening through you. If you can do that—separating yourself and trusting—you won't take on anything. You need not take on someone else's suffering. Remember, you are not the savior, God is, and that is the difference. It's about getting out of the way so that something real can happen. That's what it's about.

Q: I'm not clear about the difference between praying for people and the fact that it's not our place to know what's right for someone else.

A: Sometimes we are shown the reason for distress. I've never argued or protested that with my Source. Other times I've delved very deep in wanting to know what I was working with and finally got a response of, "It's none of your business; just keep working." And I did keep working.

There is no wrong in offering prayer for a specific affliction or asking that someone be in less discomfort or disease. You can help them feel better through the intent of your own intercessory prayer; that's not wrong. This is an opportunity to give our total self without a fight. We can have an idea what the person needs, but how can we know the perfection of it?

Q: So it doesn't matter whether you do accomplish the task through healing or through prayer?

A: Correct. It's all the same; it's all prayer anyway. But when someone says, "Oh, let me send you some energy," I say, "For what purpose? To make me feel better, to make me finish my tasks and still feel bad, or to help me just make it through this day? For what purpose is the energy you're sending? Will it make me nervous? Will I shake as if I had a cup of coffee?"

Most people will not know how to answer you. We have to wonder, "Is this just talk? Is it a chaotic prayer? Is it something that I really need, or is it energy without aid in my life?"

Prayer will be more effective if you have a focal point for channeling it into something constructive and specific. If a person has a complaint, apply it to that. Otherwise, the prayer is scattered as wasted energy without intent. If you purposefully pray for someone, be specific. Accept it, know it was done, and get out of there without looking over your shoulder to see if something happened. Otherwise, you're not letting go of it; you're still holding on to the prayer.

Q: What if you pray for the highest good for someone?

A: When you pray to God for a person, and you don't know what needs to be done, then yes, you could pray that they be taken care of in the way that is for their highest good. But don't use the highest good as an excuse to avoid your original intent of helping someone. We want them to be taken care of in a greater way, the Creator's way.

Remember, every word, every thought, and every action is our living prayer, and as we are praying and thinking and doing, we are praying for our Self and its reflection to take over.

Q: Is it possible that in a day or two the person could sabotage the work you just did because of her doubting?

A: All of us can sabotage ourselves at any time. Over the years I've watched people who were influenced to go back into older patterns of emotional and physical distress. It's difficult and oftentimes destructive for them.

But once someone has experienced healing, a seed has been planted. From that point on, any self-imposed sabotage is going to feel uncomfortable and awkward. It's like putting on an old favorite sweater from years ago that isn't your style anymore. You realize that it no longer fits, maybe it's uncomfortable to wear, and you don't like it anymore.

When we try to pick up an old pattern where we left it off, we find that we no longer have it anymore, so it feels uncomfortable. We will find a greater pattern taking its place naturally.

Q: I tend to worry about so many things. How can I help myself so that I don't worry so much anymore? My mom has also always been a worrier. How can I avoid being the same way?

A: You learned how to worry from your mother. Now you are doing the same thing. You can break this habit. You can break the mold of the conversation you grew up with. You know this is not necessary anymore. You can make a conscious choice to correct that thinking. It is only a conversation! But also think of the lessons and wisdoms you have gained from the experience.

Another thing you learned from your mom is that you loved her and wanted to be just like her in your way of thinking. It's almost a joke on you, because that's how you thought you could get love, though it really never was fulfilled, was it?

Q: Is there a possibility my thoughts of worry are harming my girls?
A: Yes, of course it is affecting their lives. You are training them just as you were trained, and you have determined what they are going to learn to be when they grow up—the same way you are! If you keep on going like this, you will definitely lead them to be the same way you are, as your mom did with you.

Why concern yourself about your children when they belong to God in the first place? Your only obligation is to house them, clothe them, feed them, support them, and love them with all your heart. The rest is up to God. All we have to learn to do is to trust God.

Q: Why is it so hard to trust? Easy to say, easy in theory, but so hard to practice.
A: Because we haven't been brought up to trust. No one has told us that we can. No one has helped to reinforce it in our lives.

Q: Is it possible to lose your abilities? What if you don't practice healing? Will you lose the ability to heal?
A: No. In the first few years of my experience, there were many times when I thought, "Oh, my God, I'm losing my power!" I have since learned that you never lose anything;

you simply put it aside. Nothing in life is ever lost. It is put aside and lies idle, to develop into something greater later. Your experiences turn it into wisdom. Sometimes we develop other priorities in life, but the option of working with these gifts is always there.

There may be a time when you are working on others but feel you are not experiencing the healing. At times I have gone to the healing circle and worked with many people, yet I felt that nothing was happening.

Meanwhile people were saying, "That is the most powerful healing circle you have ever done!" They would return the next time without their disease or injury and tell me what a powerful experience they had. I had been taken out of the way, just as you will be taken out of the way in order for healing to happen. At times it will be done without your participation. Then you may be able to get back into it with a newer, different perspective.

Q: I have a sister-in-law who is pregnant with twins. She has been told that there is something wrong with them. Last year she had a baby that died. How can I help her?

A: Visualize the outcome of perfection. Let the Creator take over, and let the Creator do what needs be done. Not what we want to do, but what the Creator wants. Most importantly, put your heart into your prayer. Visualize the perfection and say, "OK, God, here is the perfection from my sight. Let's see what you come up with." We don't know what the child coming in needs to go through, what your sister-in-law needs to go through, or how it's going to affect the world around her. These people might have something to learn too.

Because this situation affects a lot of people, we have to visualize our idea of perfection, hand it over to God, and see what happens in a greater perfection. We're usually amazed by what happens with our simple prayer of intercession. On the other hand, if you are too afraid to pray, you don't pray; then the fear is your prayer.

Q: If you are working on someone, will you always have to work on every area of blockage?
A: No, because some of the blockages, or logjams, may be subtle or at a distance from the body, which shows that the causal experience took place a long time ago. These situations may not be particularly influential in the person's life at present. Remember, some of those things you call blockages are in reality just little logjams causing disruptions, even though they may seem major to us. The person may be doing well in life without having to work on a logjam at all.

I have learned that there really are no such things as blockages, only logjams that affect each person according to their own sensitivities. If there really were a blockage, there would be no life force flowing to feed the body, and the appendage would shrivel up and fall off.

Q: Do you work with animals the same way you work with people?
A: Yes, although they're of another nature, and that would lead into a discussion about the nature of the oversoul. But animals are simpler to work with and most often do want to be understood and worked with. They often respond much more easily than humans.

9

Trust and Love

You have choice in every moment.
If you don't like the way things are,
Choose again,
Choose differently.
The choice is in the twinkling of an eye.

I. Fear No More

What is fear? Why does it have so much power over us? Fear is our negator. It grabs us and says, "Please don't trust a more conscious thinking, because if you do, I will lose you." Fear has a simple consciousness that wants to keep you away from the still, small voice of Self within. It is very afraid to lose you. Fear only knows itself.

It is not necessary to be afraid of fear, because it is only doing what it knows to do in its simple consciousness. We can picture fear as an entity that comes in and says, "Give me life. Please don't love yourself. Remember those bad, disturbing things from your past, the things that misled you!" We all have these moments many times in a day, and those moments take us out of the mind of loving ourselves.

The simple mind of fear dictates that "you should be afraid and stick with me."

Fear discounts everything and anything of a constructive, beneficial, or inspirational nature. We definitely can't hate this simple mind because it doesn't have free will. And it only knows itself. It only knows how to do one thing: to distract us and take us away from trust into mistrust.

We can do one of several things in working with this self-destructiveness: we can suppress it, while continuing to listen to it in our ignorance, or we can trust that we have a choice to do otherwise—to witness the mind as it thinks. This second choice enables us to grow and learn in experience and wisdom, and we will be able to choose more easily the next time the decision comes upon us.

We actually need fear in order to understand our choices in life. We need fear so we can recognize it and decide which way we want to proceed through experience into wisdom. Everything that doesn't inspire us or lift us up is based on fear—the conversation of the mass mind.

Fear is a separation that we have created as we have gotten far away, retreating from our Creator in the struggle of getting to know our Self. In this falling away, we look for something greater outside of ourselves: guidance, directions, stories, and personal experiences from others. But these influences don't need to dominate us. We have been continually taught to look for everything outside of ourselves. We can look for guidance outside of our Self for the rest of our lives, but won't ever find it in others' experiences; that is their experience. Nor will the Divine Source necessarily enlighten us out of nowhere; those occasions are few and far between.

Initially, as we become inquisitive, our wonderings help us to develop self-inquiry: "I wonder what is out there that is greater than me? What could I find spiritually? Who am I, and how do I fit in? What is my purpose in life?"

It's not outside; Self is inside us, always has been, and will always be. It is not separate from us; we are all a part of it, as we are integrated into Self. It is simple to agree with this statement, and yet it is often difficult to comprehend, because we have not been taught this perspective. We have been taught the perspective of fear and separateness from something greater. When we refer to God, our first tendency is to look up or away, because we have been mostly taught that God is outside of ourselves.

You are not separate from Godliness, because it is within you. Everything else is the conversation of the globalized mass mind, trying to keep you within its grasp so that you might see and believe exactly as the mass mind does.

I'm not suggesting that the worldly mind is bad or wrong, but I am suggesting that true spirituality reigns in the union, the blending, of earth and heaven.

We can gently train ourselves to pay attention to each and every thought, both the inspirational ones and the negating, awkward ones. Then we can decide which to keep and which to let go. Once you begin to be more conscious of your thoughts, you can train yourself to let go of any destructive, negating ones.

Many years ago, while living in the Order, I learned a most valuable lesson. This particular Sunday, I was alone in my room on the third floor, gazing out of the window. I was watching a fellow across the street on a dolly underneath the front of his car; the tire was off, and his feet were hanging out. As I gazed at this activity, my thoughts began to wander. I had a fantasy that the small metal jack would not hold the massive weight of this car. The story I was making up in my head had the metal wheel falling and cutting him in two. My mind was in tunnel vision, mesmerized and with no conscious way out. Then one of the sisters burst into the room and started yelling at me: "What are you doing?" I didn't understand what she was talking about and looked quizzically at her. She came up to me at the window and sternly said, "Look, look at what you were doing!" I turned to the fellow under the car. Just then he pulled the dolly out, and the car fell. He would have been severely injured or killed.

It shocked me! I had to try to understand what had just happened. This was important to me. Could this be real? Did I do this? Or did I just see this coming into manifestation? So many questions I had.

Here is an exercise that will teach you to purposefully focus as well as to break many destructive patterns.

Try this wonderful and simple exercise for three days in a row. Do not add anything to this exercise; do not think about it or analyze or critique what might be happening. If we do, we're not doing the exercise, and the mind is going elsewhere.

Over a period of three days, and starting the exercise each day upon awakening: simply count the number of negating, destructive thoughts on your fingers in one day. Just count them one at a time. Watch how they diminish in number, and watch their power diminish. Of course, it takes concentration and practice: this is learning the ability to focus. You can also do this exercise to reduce the things that have become fearful and negating in your life.

WHAT IS SABOTAGE?

Sabotage is that which creates doubt in the soundness of our lives. It is what we do to eliminate our trust in knowing that everything really is OK. Our tainted vision of life keeps us from seeing this fact. We tend to sabotage ourselves at every opportunity available. We negate ourselves through our lack of faith in our own control, integrity, and capacity to survive. This is completely unnecessary.

Most of our sabotages extend from our childhood experiences. You can blame them on past life experiences or anything else. If you do, then you think of them as carryovers from a previous life and possibly the ones before that. What difference does it make? The sabotage is still happening in this time and place. It is still registered in the memory and information that we emanate internally and externally through our morphic field today. Similarly, we can work with it in this life and in this moment. If you recognize that there was some event that led you to feel how you feel today, even if you don't remember exactly how it started, you can choose to work it out differently. Why not go ahead and work it out now?

It takes a simple recognition that there was something that helped you feel about things the way you do and led you to become who you are, what you are, and why you are. These causal events built you and helped you to develop into the person you are today. There is no need to carry them on. At any given moment, we have a choice—free will—to change or sustain anything, including any think-ing process or psychological pattern, even those pertaining to physical dilemmas.

For example, if we find ourselves worrying in a way that keeps us preoccupied and produces physical distur-bances in our body, we can recognize when it was that we learned to worry in this fashion. That's when the conversa-tion of worry started for us. It may have been many years ago. Perhaps another child wouldn't play with us, and we decided that we would always have to be worried that the other children wouldn't play with us, because we weren't worthy enough.

Maybe our dad kept telling us that we weren't well behaved enough to play outside. When we finally did go out to play, there was a fear that inhibited us from being accepted or participating. We were the ones that made that decision and conversation, which have followed us all these years. When we objectively recognize that there was a sin-gle event that led into a single decision about our life that we made that did not really have a basis, or was a misun-derstanding or misinterpretation, we are free of it. We can let it go. But we have to walk through it within ourselves and recognize the emotional conversations that we had as a child and are still living in.

You choose your place in the world. You decide what you wish to sustain and what you wish to change in your world.

The world around you, the environment you live in, even your friends and family, may encourage you to stay as you are. They encourage you not to choose a different way of looking at anything. They are comfortable with you the way you already are—even if you are being self-destructive.

They expect it from you even if they don't express it: you are simply validating their own beliefs about you. They too can be sources of sabotage if you believe they are keeping you secure but entrapped in that world of self-destruction. If you can let these things go and let in the clarity of the Divinity Within, you will stop reacting to and resisting to the world around you, instead choosing your place in the world with clarity of mind.

II. Downtime Is Our Time

Downtimes are given to us in order to force us to take a break. They are times for us to learn, integrate our most immediate experiences, and grow in various aspects of our lives.

Downtimes may last five minutes, a day, a week, or over several months. I've had periods last up to three months. During one of those extended times, I thought I had lost everything. I thought that healing had been taken from me; I had served my purpose and nothing more was going to be happening in my life.

I realized this wasn't so when a woman approached me to work on her. I thought everything was gone and nothing would happen. I was prepared to apologize for being unable to help anyone anymore. Several weeks later, that same woman approached me, apologizing that she hadn't gotten back to me sooner to express how the healing had changed her life.

Boy, I was wrong. That became one of the most powerful healing experiences I have ever had. I have had hundreds of downtimes, but I have also learned to trust that they were developmental periods when I could watch myself being taken out of the way for something more to develop and manifest.

I have learned to trust in my downtimes. You could trust yours as well. Realize that there is always chaos, because something is changing, and we cannot have change without chaos. Then and only then will the downtimes occur less frequently. It is as though you become friends with the downtime and no longer fear it.

Again, downtimes are handed to us so that we can integrate prior developments. Downtimes are not given to throw us into depression; they are times of experience and understanding turning into wisdom.

WHEN YOU ARE FEELING ILL

This is a great exercise when you're starting to feel sick.

When I begin to have a sense of being sick with a headache, cold or something else, I've learned to imagine that I can see a stream of consciousness that is coming into my head. This stream of consciousness helps me to realize I should be feeling bad, with a cold or the flu or whatever. Then I mentally step back a foot or two and imagine that stream passing right by me. This is when I realize that I don't have that bad feeling for a moment or two—that is, until I start thinking about it again and it finds me again. Then I do the same thing in my mind again and again, until I fully let go of the expectation of feeling unwell. You can adapt this basic method and make it more vivid visually.

I always like to be creative with spirituality and change things around, not doing the same thing forever. Here's a similar technique that I have utilized: if I begin to be aware that I am starting to get a cold or the flu, I might imagine a stream that represents the cold coming into my head (from some outside source). I'll say to it, "No. Wait here" (directing it to right outside of me). "I'll be right back. You can come and sit or float next to me and move in and put up your pictures, light your fire, put up your tent . . . you can do all the things you want to do. But I'll be right back. You wait here. I can't accept you right now, because I have something else to do." Then I'll simply walk away from it to do something else. Try this with the intention of not accepting this cold— ever. Leave it behind.

Remember all the times you have thought, "Oh! I'm starting to feel sick, but I can't get sick right now because I have so much going on." And you don't get sick at that time! But the minute what you were working on is done, bam! You get sick. The same is true of mothers with sick children. When the child is sick, the mother needs to be there to take care of the child. She is saying in her mind, "I can't get sick! I have to take care of my child!" Often when the child is on the upswing, the mother does come down with the cold or flu.

In both these cases, you asked for the sickness to wait until you had the time for it, but you accepted it back into your system later; you let it in to stay with you. Realize that you were the one who put the illness on hold to begin with, so you can continue to do this indefinitely.

You need your downtime in order to be cleansed and grow. But you do not need to have the illness or symptoms ordinarily associated with it to accomplish this goal. In fact, you are going through cleansings all the time. It is just that we resort to feeling ill to allow ourselves to take the time to regroup spiritually, mentally, emotionally, and physically.

Our conversations saying we need to be debilitated or sick are prayers that we're relating to the Universal Mind, the Creator, in order to have a break in life. These thoughts have constantly reinforced themselves over many years.

Give yourself permission to take voluntary downtimes. Take the time to meditate, sleep, relax, eat right, read a book, paint a picture, work with clay, work in the yard, weave a basket, knit something, have a good meal, or exercise. You don't have to get sick in order to have downtime. You know where we all learned to originally accept these patterns, right? Consider this discussion carefully, and see how it relates to your life.

In one of my Order experiences, I walked in the chapel one day and saw Brother David kneeling before the altar with his arms extended in total supplication. He was praying out loud to God to make him pure. Of course I grimaced, backstepped, and quietly slipped out of the room. Later that day in a hallway, about five feet from me, the teacher was there confronting David, asking why he so often had a cold that would last him for weeks at a time. Then the teacher walked away. A couple of days later, Brother David's cold was gone. I remembered Brother David and his weird prayer. I now saw what he was doing to himself to be pure: he had stayed in the constant state of a cold ever since I had known him. This analogy helped me to see at that time what our prayers or desires can do in our moment to moment living.

Then I thought, "Oh my goodness! All my life I've had a cold every three or four months. And, if the teacher could call Brother David on that and it stopped, why can't I use this same principle on myself?" So I pictured the cold as a mindset pattern, a consciousness, that cleansed my body.

I talked to that consciousness and let it know there were to be no more symptoms of runny nose, headache, or sore throat. Well, three months later, I knew and could sense a cold, but there were no symptoms!

It wasn't until ten or fifteen years later that I did get a cold. It was wintertime, and I was in Nashville, on an escalator going down. A tall fellow behind me sneezed all over the back of my head and neck. I knew then that I had the cooties! Boy, did I get the creeps. That night sickness came over me. But I thought, "Oh my, I haven't been sick for years. So why not let this little cold play itself out? After all, it's just a little cleansing." That night, I kept getting sicker and sicker. Then I began to suffer with a bad sore throat and massive headache; I was constantly blowing my nose as I shoved Kleenex into it. That was enough. I begged God to help me or take my life—whatever it took to get rid of this cold. Finally, after falling asleep, the next morning I awoke to many fewer symptoms.

DEVELOPING ASSURANCE IN HEALING

With time and practice, you will develop skill and expertise in healing. The techniques presented here are tools to aid in your development. The more you practice, the more adept you will become at handling your tools.

Please understand, though, that these exercises and tools won't necessarily be easy to use. But also understand that the way we learned to live is the more difficult way to live. These tools help us find a simpler, easier, and more natural way, without many of the typical resistances. The more you practice, the more confident you will become, and you will see faster results. Healing will become a more conscious part of you. Every person has healing abilities to varying degrees, and everyone is unique in their process. Soon after days or weeks of practice, we notice that these things have become part of our life without any further need to practice.

Be bold and step out into what you have learned. Very few people have recognized themselves within the living philosophy and reality of this kind of healing. You have learned to call on the Creator, the Divinity Within, your Self, without getting bogged down or sabotaged in the process.

THE CONSTANT FLOW OF GIVING

We heal ourselves as we heal others. Whatever we see projected in any other person is mirrored in our own lives. When we work on another person, we are in the process of recognizing this fact. The mass mind says that we cannot possibly help another person until we heal ourselves first. Not true! As we put our heart into what we are doing, we are not only affecting someone else but ourselves as well. It is the heart that really matters in anything we pursue.

As we begin to help ourselves, we can also begin to help others.

The mind of Godliness is the ecosystem of all creation. It is unceasing and continually unfolding, constantly in flow. It is within us, and it knows only a flow of constant giving and finding its level of acceptance within us as we allow this to happen. It is good, and it is within.

We can do anything we want with the energy of thought; we can easily use it for destruction if we choose, and we will live with the effects. We can also use this energy to improve our lives and those of others and manifest things much greater than we believed possible. In either case, we are still living within the law of cause and effect. The world we want is the one we get. This too is the law of cause and effect. After all, it's only energy.

Everything in life is your stepping stone. Everything is there for your growth and development. As long as you realize that these healing practices are just tools, you cannot hurt people. If you do something in innocence, out of love, the other person will be taken care of. If you do something to hurt others or with selfish intent, repercussions will always follow. This too is of the law of cause and effect.

If you go into healing with the intent of helping out with selflessness and love from the heart, without controlling any situation, a greater mind will take care of it for you. It is done. You too will be taken care of.

Our purpose is to be more conscious of that still, small voice within, which empowers us. As we do, we subordinate our self to a greater mind and allow it to operate more consciously in our own lives. We learn to interact and participate in the ultimate act of love, in harmony and oneness with all others and our Self. Through the experience of being objective and letting Godliness express itself through us in our healing practices, we move into the domain of loving and being loved. This love is creative and protective. It softens the heart. We are given the opportunity to love ourselves. Then compassion comes upon us.

THE TIME IS NOW

We must not be stopped by the resistance the world has imposed upon us.

There is something within us that is always waiting for us to honor and acknowledge it. This thing inside, called

Self, is alive and well. We are just shells for it. Self is with us at every moment, talking to us, guiding us, and directing us. Through intuition, we communicate with the Divine as we learn to stay true to the guidance and direction that it shares with us.

In the moments that we awaken in our realization, we avoid following the way of the rest of the world. At these times, the mass mind will pounce on us in order to get us back to its way of living. It will throw dilemmas, dramas, and traumas at us as we move further into a spiritual, more conscious life. You will become worried again, angry, fearful, sad, and confused. You will also think, "Well, that spiritual experience was nice for a time, but now I have to get back to the 'real' world." You will be tempted to get out of this newer, higher state and turn back to the old way.

As you practice trusting that everything's OK, you realize that Self is more powerful than anything or anyone else, and you will be able to survive spiritually and physically in this brave new world. You will be able to create a balance between what you now know as spiritually and the "real" world.

The more you practice this, the easier it becomes. You will find that you can do it, but only if you trust that everything is OK. Accept this trust. Don't let the doubts slip in; catch them and recognize them. If you fall prey to them, they will be fulfilled once again. The most wonderful part of this is that we're given more opportunities than we can imagine to catch ourselves in our failings and make another choice.

Now is the time to start trusting. It took your whole life to get you to this point. Now you are here to work it out by becoming conscious that you can give to ourselves and others, especially when they are hurt or in emotional distress.

I hope that your understanding of what you may call Creator, God, Universe, or Self is alive and well within you. This book is here to show you this truth and reinforce it in you. We truly carry a piece of this Divinity, Godliness, the Nameless One within us, and its fulfillment is waiting for each of us.

10

Meditation Resources

This chapter contains some phrases you can use in meditation, as well as material for two longer meditations: the Flow of Life and the Divine Self Meditation.

Phrases Used for Meditation

Choose one phrase each week for meditating (not more than twenty minutes at a sitting). Use one phrase for the entire week, during the day, as you can set up the pattern to contemplate the phrase. Then go to the next phrase the following week.

By the end of one or two weeks, you will have noticed an alchemical change created within you, which will affect your perceptual and emotional understanding.

1. Love is inspiring and illuminating; therefore it gives light and life.

2. The Light has a consciousness; it has an intelligence. It knows what to do with me or without me.

3. Every word, every thought, every action is my living prayer.

4. Self is always there, waiting to guide and direct me.

5. Divinity is within me, waiting. I need only listen.

6. Go forth and heal in love, without judgment.

7. I feel the love of Divinity within me.

8. I know what to do.

9. To see the Divinity in others is the only way.

10. I cease to think of God as external. God is within me.

The Breath of God

Read this exercise in its entirety before beginning. Study the text and determine what you are looking for as a result of focused breathing. Place a pad of paper and a pen or pencil nearby or on your lap. Once you have done the above, you may begin.

Imagine yourself breathing in the breath of God.

Breathe it all the way in through your sinus cavities and throughout your skull.

Breathe the breath of God in through your nostrils, all the way in,

And begin to feel the tingling aliveness

Of your nerve endings, touching everything within you.

Feel the alertness, the excitement in your body.

Notice how the bones of your head feel.

The light that you are sensing is actually becoming clearer.

If you feel it in your skull,

You are not really feeling it in your actual bones,

But in the layer of tissue on the surface of your bones that have the nerve endings.

This is merely the place where you feel the sensations.

Keep your eyes closed and continue breathing.

Breathe in deeply through your nostrils all the way to the bottom of your lungs,

And exhale slowly through your mouth.

You will feel a sense of flow within you.

Your body is emanating energy.

It is the life force within you.

It is your electrical, magnetic bond, which keeps all the cells together.

Imagine the tingling is caused by the cells coming alive.

Smell the energy as it emanates from you.

Keep coming back to sensing the energy.

It almost pulses off your body in waves.

It's very subtle.

Tune into this.

Register what it feels like.

Find yourself going deeper into yourself.

Sense the energy coming off your body.

Conscious awareness is being consciously aware

Of what is going on around you and within you.

Sense the pulses of energy coming from you.

If you perceive something, slightly open your eyes,

Or keep them closed, if you can,

And write the perception on your pad of paper.

Keep going deeper within yourself.

Continue with the breathing; notice if it has changed.

Perhaps you notice the slowness of it and the lack of breathing.

It is the breath of God nourishing you.

Now, with your eyes still closed, starting with your feet,

Slowly scan your body.

Use your internal senses.

You will discover areas of discomfort or areas that need work.

Slowly work your way up,

Exploring your body in its entirety.

Say to it, "Talk to me. Tell me or show me what you want to show me or tell me."

Keep going back to your body.

If you perceive something, write it down.

As you scan your body, repeat, "Talk to me. Tell me or show me what you want to show me or tell me."

In your mind, listen to the silence,

And pay attention to the pictures,

Sounds, and colors that come forth.

Focus on this scanning process while working your way up your body

Looking for information, as you say,

"Talk to me. Tell me or show me what you want to show me or tell me."

Practice quickening this process

By moving your awareness more rapidly.

Stop at any spot where you feel dysfunction.

Keep talking to it to gain insight.

You will perceive answers.

When you have worked your way all the way up,

Slowly open your eyes. Slowly open your eyes.

Read what you have written.

Does it make sense to you?

Does it provide you with a different understanding?

The Flow of Life: A Spiritual Focus Exercise

The purpose of contemplative imagery is to help you to become more at peace with your Self and to be healthier. It also will help you to become more spiritual in your focus and to experience of your oneness with the God Self within.

This exercise might be somewhat difficult the first or second time you attempt it. Don't trouble yourself if you start to feel saturated by all that you experience. Only go as far as you comfortably can. It is wise not to overdo it. Then go back to it again later that day, or the next.

If you do not have the accompanying audio of this exercise, ask a partner to read the exercise to you with a steady cadence, or record an audio for yourself.

❧ 1 ❧

Begin to quiet down inside.

Let your eyelids drop and relax.

Breathe slowly and evenly—

In through your nose and out through your mouth.

Slowly and evenly.

Begin to feel the flow of life through out your body.

As it begins to flow,

You begin to get in touch with the flow.

From your heart, know that

You can feel a sense of love—

The Love that the Nameless One has for you.

We know that this Love is hidden within the deepest
   recesses of our hearts.
Let the love slowly come out from your heart
Let the love flow into the surrounding areas in your chest,
And it begins to spread outward.
Know that in our natural spiritual state,
We too are composed of effervescent light,
Filled with its joy of being,
Naturally fulfilled within the greater Love,
And that initially we came forth from that Love.
This life comes from within the Divine Mind,
Of pure life and consciousness,
From the mind of Love.

The clear, euphoric feeling that we are sensing
Is a result of opening the heart and mind to it,
Trusting it, allowing it,
And allowing your true Self
To be fulfilled from the Love within.
And it is filling and being fulfilled within you.
Get comfortable with your Self,
And let your Self become a friend to you,
Watch yourself becoming more quiet.
Allow Self to love you.
Let the flow of Love express its Self in you—
Naturally and without your interference.
Breathing slowly and gently
That this flow might move freely in you.
In its expression of love in you.

Allow all the thoughts of other things, other times, and
    other places
To just flow away
And watch them dissipate into nothingness,
That you may begin to focus on your true Self.
The feeling and the senses within
Sense the fear of doing this exercise,
Of letting go of everything else.
Watch the fear melt.

Allow your body to relax,
Feeling your muscles and feet,
Arms and hands as they keep dropping,
Let them drop even more
As you watch the tensions and worries of the day,
Watching them flow slowly away
Out from your awareness and your body.
Feeling the flow of life flow through you
As the fear lessens within you,
And the Godliness within you becomes more manifest.

❧ 2 ❧

Begin to feel the slight electrical charge as it feels prickly
In your hands and in your feet and below your scalp.
Focus on your hips,
And focus on the pelvic area of bones and muscles
And small organs within.
Visualize a nerve network, almost like roots
Growing through the muscles, the bones of your thighs,
    and your legs,

As they develop and search for their source of life,
Just as roots do for water,
Flowing and searching and reaching down into the earth
As a conscious network of veins and capillaries,
Sending the roots down through your body and
Spreading down into the raw, fertile earth
As they branch out in search of life—
Through the earth, and growing deeper—
The roots of a mighty tree.
Imagine your roots going down through the many layers
    of the earth,
Down through the layers of the soil, through the sand,
The silt, the gravel, and the stone—
Reaching deep into the earth towards its core.
Know that the entire earth contains magnetic energies.
These energies are also naturally a part of you.
Begin to feel the magnetic energies of your body,
To draw upon them freely.
Know also that the consciousnesses of the earth energies
Are magnetically attracted to you too,
And that your body feels and knows that too.
Feel your roots growing downward,
Moving through the depths of the earth until
They begin to enter the periphery of a mass—
As though the mass carries a massive presence
Of fire and magnetism.
As your roots just begin to break
Through the periphery of the mass,
These roots also begin to connect
With this mass of energy within the earth.
You begin to sense and see

That it is a deep shade of bloodred and gold energy.
And it carries the sound of soft and powerful rumblings.

Try to perceive this energy mass vibrating
Eight times in a second.
And as it vibrates, it helps us to keep our own body's cycle
Near a rate of sixteen pulses in a minute.
Watch it and feel it as it feeds your pulse of life.
This mass vibrates at the same frequency as a
Naturally healthy body.

As your roots are enmeshed in the mass of energy
And become one with the mass,
They automatically attune
To the vibrational pattern of this mass of energy.
This mass is the earth's blood,
The flow that sustains all life on earth.

Pull this bloodred and gold of the earth
Up into and through your roots and nerves.
Watching the energy as it moves up through this network,
Slowly at first,
Begin to feel the sensation of the bottoms of your feet
Wanting to open wider
As though they have vents
Thirsting for this life.
As you begin to trust this energy,
Feel it freely flowing more into your feet,
The more your vents open, the less fearful you will be.
Imagine yourself wanting more of it.

Feel the magnetic bloodred and gold flowing into your
    ankles,
Up to your legs, up through your thighs,
And into the muscles that bind your hips.
Feel it flowing into your belly,
And slowly into your solar plexus area,
And then permeating your chest cavity,
Flowing slowly
Into your heart.

From your heart through your arms
And from your arms as they fill,
This life flow permeates your shoulders
And up into your throat, and then into your spine.
From top to the bottom and back up again
Into your head
As the mass slowly swirls within you,
As it gives you life.

Feel your heart fill
With this bloodred and gold energy of the earth.
Notice the feelings that this magnetic energy creates in
    your body
As it brings you to greater realities and sensations,
A different understanding.
Notice the sensations.
You may be feeling a gravitational pull
Towards this source of life from the earth.
Allow this earth energy
To gently warm the inside of your chest and heart.
As you begin to feel it,

Feel this energy,
As it gently and pleasantly warms your chest,
As it flows throughout your body and heart, in warmth.
As you feel your heart pumping in the strength of the flow,
Feel the warmth of the flow of the energy moving through
    you.

⇜ 3 ⇝

Turn your attention to the top of your head.
Picture a slightly glazed window in the top of your head
And look through the window outward.
Try to decipher what you are seeing as you look outward.
Watch as the window's glaze dissipates to clarity.
And see that there is no longer any obstruction,
Feel the flow of light,
Its waves and its particles of energy
Beginning to flow through you.
Envision this light as clear, effervescent, and glistening,
And rest in its wisdom.

It will help you to become more aware
Of the manifestation of Godliness within you,
Slowly bringing the flow of the clean, clear, effervescent
    light
Into the top your head,
And slowly down through your spine,
Imagining your spine
As it is filled with this clear healing light.
The more you allow it to manifest within you,
And permeate you, exhilarate you,
The more you notice how different you feel.

Experience this healing light filling your entire being
As it begins to freely flow throughout your body
Without resistance.
As the healing light pervades your entire being,
Also watch as it extends outward from your body
And around you, into the energy fields which you generate.

Continue to bring this light through the top of your head,
Down through your spine.
Notice that your heart is also full of light.
Sense how it feels as the light fills and nourishes your heart.
Let the sensations expand.
Allow it to completely fill your chest cavity,
Saturating you
With clear, effervescent light.

❧ 4 ❧

Once again,
Pull in the deep bloodred and gold earth energy
And its magnetism
Up through your feet,
Up through your legs, and up into your pelvic area,
Moving towards the stomach and into the chest—
Bringing it more into your heart and saturating it.
Try to visualize and imagine the mixing of both these
    energies,
Of the clean, clear, effervescent healing light
And the deep bloodred and gold earth energy—
Both swirling within the heart, blending together,
As the swirling mixture within your chest
Fills your heart.

Watch as the valves of your heart open fully,
Distributing the mixture of magnetism and light
As it is carried into the vessels, the veins, and the
    capillaries,
Into the cells of your body,
Throughout the wholeness of your body.

Send this blend of energy down through your arms and legs
As it flows to the very tips of your fingers and toes.
And you feel your fingers and toes and scalp tingle
With a slight electrical sensation.

❧ 5 ☙
Now, silently and slowly, bring your hands together,
Barely touching,
And gently rub your hands.
Pull your hands about one inch apart,
Barely touching, palm to palm.
As you keep your hands still in that position,
Continue to visualize
Pulling through your feet the earth's magnetism
With the electrically charged energy of light
Flowing through you
As they mix together.
Breathe deeply and slowly,
In through your nose,
Down to the lowest part of your belly,
Slowly, out through your mouth.

Slightly and slowly pull your hands apart,
Only three to five inches at the most,

Feeling the energy surging,
Filling your hands and your wrists.
Feel the small mass of energy between your hands,
At its periphery,
As you move your hands
Slightly closer and slightly further apart.
It is not necessary to overdo it.

Feel the magnetic pull of energies between your hands,
As you bring your hands slightly closer—
The attraction.
And feel the repulsion of the pulse at the further distance
As you slightly separate the hands.

Very gently, feel this energy on the surface of your hands.
Feel how it, in some way, might be affecting you.
Get to know it a little.
Try to understand it.
This is the life force that you carry fully embodied within.
This energy of Light is your gift, your very life.
In times of sickness and distress
It deteriorates slightly and needs to be resupplied.
When it is totally depleted
Through the lack of creativity and oxygenation
And blood flow in the body and brain, we cease to exist.

This energy of light is in every cell, between every cell.
It also forms your electrical matrix within and around
    your body
And extends outward into and through the universe.
It is the energy field that carries

The information of your life into the aura,
The information of the morphic field
Within and around you.
Take a moment to perceive it.
Now gently place your hands on your lap.
Focus again on pulling up the deep red and gold energies
    of the earth.
From that mass of energy deep within the earth,
Into your body and again filling your heart
Focus again on the luminous electrically charged light
Flowing into your head
And also flowing into your heart.

As you watch the swirling motion inside your heart,
Warming, opening, and melting the layers of veils
That have been created to hide the Love within—
Veils of what you thought and have been taught
Was protecting your Self from the world of hurt.

Feel the love of the radiant sun,
In all its magnificence,
And its manifestation of the Godliness,
The Divinity Within,
Bringing life into your heart.
Feel it fill your heart,
And your body,
And the many fields that emanate from you and around you.
Try to imagine how it might feel to you,
Living within the mind of God—
The unlimited magnitude of the information
That might be offered to you.

6

Experience the gentleness, the joy,
The reality of this world,
Knowing now that we have a choice
Of which world we wish to live in.
Take a moment to enjoy this.
Try to feel it with all your heart.
Open your heart.
This is your living Self,
Unconditionally loving you and giving to you,
In the way that you always have wanted to feel
And know its love.
Feel its love within you,
Expressing its love to you.
And when you get ready to come back to the room
Slowly open your eyes—
And bring this Love back with you.
Slowly open your eyes.
And bring its Love back with you.
Begin to come back now.
When you are ready,
Slowly come back
And slowly open your eyes.

The Divine Self Meditation

For best results with the Divine Self Meditation, listen to my audio recording *Divine Self* while you are doing this exercise. It will take you through the practice step by step so that you can experience a greater adventure. If you don't have a copy of this recording, you can read the material below aloud and record it yourself, or you can have a partner read it aloud to you.

I was introduced to this exercise while in the Order. It is an ancient exercise using the image of an egg. In ancient writings, the egg represents the one who has attained self-realization. It has always been the symbol of truth. This exercise is designed to bring you to a conscious atonement—at-one-ment—at one with health, clarity of mind, deep visualization, peace, and awareness of the light within. It will enable you to open to contact with Self or the conscious Divinity Within—to the Nameless One, as mystics of old called it, and its embryonic state, which composes the universe. It will also connect you to the fluidity that carries the mind of the Nameless One dwelling within.

Conscious practice of this exercise for twenty minutes a day for only two weeks will enhance your awareness within of the Divinity Within—Self or the Nameless One. Through Self, all things will be shown.

As a result of this exercise, you will experience an overall sense of well-being and peacefulness within, as well as improvement in health and well-being. Within two weeks of practice, you may also see images and experience changes in your mental perceptions. If you are in a darkened room, you may notice a slight glow, a light around yourself, during or after the exercise. This is a natural result of practicing this meditation.

This exercise is your opportunity to attain self-improvement and should not be taken lightly. The more you practice, the more you will be transformed. It will quicken your mental and spiritual growth and even your reality.

Your spiritual senses will be internalized through heightened awareness of the Divinity Within.

Use moderation in practicing this exercise. It should not be done more than twice a day or more than five days in each week.

Let us begin.
Sit in a relaxed position, in a straight-backed chair, feet
    flat on the ground.
Let your arms drop, and then let your hands drop.
Let's clear your mind now.
First, breathe in slowly and gently
Through your nose and out through your mouth.
It is written that God, the Nameless One,
Breathed through the nostrils of man and woman
And gave them life.
If this is true,
Then we are breathing in the breath of God.
Breathe in slowly through your nose
And gently out through your mouth.
Breathe deeply down to the lower abdomen.
With each exhalation, feel all tension leaving
And your body becoming more relaxed.
You will find yourself
Becoming lighter and more euphoric.
You might feel a slight electrical charge
Silently flowing through the terminals of your fingers and
    your toes
And right below the surface of your scalp.
These feelings are the fluid of the spirit moving through
    you.

There is no need to consciously let it flow out of you.
Feel it well up from within you.

Continue with a very slow breathing pattern throughout
    the exercise.
Imagine a slow series of waves
Moving through your head.
Become comfortable with the waves;
Let them flow freely.
This will allow your cellular consciousness
To shift without interference.

Now be aware of the waves
As they slowly move downward
Into your throat and through your spine.
Downward through your chest,
Down through your arms and hands,
From your chest to your lower abdomen.
Feel the waves move from your lower abdomen
To your ligaments and muscles that bind your hips
As the waves surge through your legs and down to your feet.
Allowing the fluid of the spirit to well up from within,
Imagine these waves going through your entire body
From head to toe.
Your whole body is becoming more relaxed and lighter
    and clearer.
Stay conscious of your breathing.
Feel the clarity and lightness in your entire body.

Visualize yourself within an oval-shaped egg
Filled with clean, clear, effervescent, bubbly light.

Subtle light is emanating from you.
This light creates a shell around you,
A shell composed entirely of light.
As you watch this experience,
You are actually seeing your true Self
Emanating light.
Now imagine yourself standing
Or sitting or even suspended there.
Your experience of this will be unique to you.
Through your nostrils
Continue to breathe in slowly
The breath of God,
The breath of the Nameless One of the Universe,
And slowly out through your mouth
Through which the Word comes forth.
Slowly become one
With the light of the shell around you.
Watch the light from within
As it pulsates outwards.
Focus on the pulsation.
Watch the particles of light become illuminated
Just as a match flares into brightness.

In that moment, the tiny particles of light
Create a series of waves.
You become enlightened within the form you carry.
Watch your arms reach up into it.
Feel the sensations of the light
Carry through your being of clear form.
Feel it flowing freely.
Now step out. Move out of the shell.

Be aware of the light from your form.
Feel the emanations from within you
Coming out through you.
Feel the joy of its expression around you.
Very slowly, move in and out of the shell.
This will help you adapt to it and it to you.
The shell too has a living consciousness.
Experience the freedom and joy and health
Of what you truly are,
What you see inside and outside the shell.
Experience the peace, quietude, intelligence, wisdom, and
    consciousness
Of the subtle light and its life that gives you life.

Now go back into the shell.
Slowly bring this consciousness into your physical being.
Remember your experience from within.
Feel it, sense it, and let it live still within you.
As you do, you bring this consciousness back with you
Into the atmosphere that emanates around you.
Slowly come back.
As you do, bring this consciousness with you.
Slowly come back.
Slowly open up your eyes.
Sit still for a few moments.

Take a little time to recuperate, flitting between earth
and heaven, and allow yourself to come back. Stand up
slowly and move around.

11

Guide to Exercises

This quick reference guide provides you with access to many of the meditations and exercises given in the rest of the book. The exercises presented are to be worked with without emotional reaction. To have the greatest effect, they should be enacted with objectivity.

Focus on Yourself

Here is an exercise that may be difficult to practice at first, but will have definite long-term benefits:

Find and choose one habit that you dislike most about yourself. Keep going back in your memory to remember when it happened last. Then go back as far as you can to possibly find out when it might have started, its initial process, and when you first began applying it habit in your life.

Then ask yourself, "Why did it start?" Wonder about what might have influenced you to take on that habit. Wait until you remember one or more causes for it. (*Remember-ing* means bringing the members—pieces—of your memory back together into view).

By seeing, hearing, feeling or knowing, objectively relive the dynamic sense that within you will reveal your answer. This only takes the desire to do the exercise. It will give you an understanding of how this particular habit has affected you.

You will find yourself reflecting on the current manifestation in your thinking. When this happens, take what you have just perceived, and watch the situation unfold *objectively*. Review that dynamic remembrance; observe it as if it were the first time that you were experiencing it.

See if you can find the primary causal moment in your life that led to you to carry the habit with you, contributing to who you are, why you are, and what you are today.

If indeed you have found the causal moment, watch what happens as it is revealed within. In that moment, a healing has taken place. The experience could change your life for the rest of your life!

Your transformation has only just begun. It will change your mental perceptions and your emotional reactions to them. Your thinking processes may also have produced biological effects that have manifested in bodily dysfunction.

This exercise builds your ability to watch and perceive in sundry ways in order to go through your own metamorphosis. The idea is to watch the process objectively, without becoming involved in the emotions, dramas, and traumas you witness. This is not possible unless you try this as a simple exercise and realize that in reality, there is nothing to fear. The truth does not kill us or harm us; nor can it make us sick. The truth helps you to see yourself and thereby sets you free.

Conscious Awareness I

Please read this in its entirely before you begin.

Stand facing a partner. Look your partner in the eyes and keep watching them. Look deep into his or her eyes.

Consciously stop whatever mental conversations you may be having at the moment. Stop the thinking process that is wrapped up in the conversation. Go within yourself and see what is really being said and done within you. Watch the other person think.

Try that for just a moment. That is all that is needed—a moment in your life.

Go within yourself. You will see that moment has no specific time or duration. Watch your partner while focusing within you. Surrender to your Self for this insight. Communicate with it in your mind. As you surrender yourself, begin to feel its warmth flowing freely through you. This process will take you into a new, more real conscious awareness. This awareness may last for a few seconds at first, but as you practice this, these moments turn into minutes.

Feeling Love

With all your heart and soul, feel the love coming forth from within you. Consciously talk to it from inside your head. Express to it your need to love and listen as it tells you of its love you and its desire for your love. Realize this love as a close friend. Become aware of it. You can almost touch it. This is what awareness is. You are taking it on; you are clothing yourself with it. That's awareness. Let it flow through you. Let the love live through you. Let it love you. Feel its love, and imagine the essence of that love as if it were a presence around you, hugging and permeating you. Let it finally express its love for you, which you have never felt before. Now slowly come on back.

The Retrospection Exercise

This retrospection exercise helped me learn to have concentrated focus.

It is to be done when you lie down to go to sleep for the night.

Have your eyes closed or open; it doesn't matter. See yourself in what you are doing at that moment. Then begin to go back through your day, remembering one fairly significant event that happened right before bedtime. It can be any event. Don't get wrapped up in it. Imagine you are watching a movie when you are recalling this event. Perhaps it was a conversation or an action that led to a significant outcome.

Now go to another fairly significant event that happened prior to the first one you remembered—something that was upsetting, something you argued about, something you said or thought of either a positive or negative nature. Then remember something that happened prior to that, working your way all the way back to when you first awakened that day.

At first, you may not be able to put things in their exact order, but that doesn't really matter. It's not necessary to dwell on anything that you haven't done perfectly. That only sabotages the purpose of the exercise.

You will achieve a more precise order as you practice this exercise day after day. Your memory will bloom magnificently, and you will develop a knowing that will be an important part of you for years to come.

At the end of the exercise, take everything you recognized in that retrospection and say, "OK God, Creator, here are all the good things and not so good things that happened in my day. Here's the great me, and the not so great me. Here are all the events, no matter what they were. Take them all, gather them all together and cleanse them for me. Wash the whole of it for me: scrub it, launder it, reshape it, and put it into its place so I can see how it may now turn out the next day." Then watch as a hand comes into your head and pulls those thoughts out.

If you let go of these events, whether they are important or trivial, giving them to Source, they are no longer yours. If you try to conjure them back up again, that means you're not willing to turn them over yet. What you accept is what you get.

Conscious Awareness II

To foster conscious awareness, try this exercise for one minute.

Sit quietly and imagine what it might be like to think of nothing.

Now notice all the conversations you're having in your mind.

Consciously stop yourself from any of these conversations for moments at a time.

Imagining that you can stop yourself from being wrapped up in your many conversations, just watch yourself; observe yourself.

Notice the thinking process and all the deviations that are wrapped up in your conversation.

Next imagine watching yourself as another person talking. Try this for just one minute, as often as you like.

Concentrate on what is really happening in your thinking.

This is all that is needed: one minute in your life. There will be several times in that one minute when you might lose focus. You will notice how busy and active things seem around you. But as you notice this busyness, you observe yourself as if in slow motion.

Stopping Thought

Another one-minute exercise: You may think you have no control over what you say or think. But actually we can stop our thoughts in their tracks. We can decide whether we want to think or say or do any given thing. We can change it any time we want; that is our free will. We will understand these things are true if we can realize, that our word, thought, and action are alive and creates.

You will soon become aware that one minute does not in actuality have a specific time element or duration: there is no time in the nonlinear world.

Practicing this exercise with desire will bring wonderful results. Your ability to focus and concentrate will increase exponentially in just two weeks.

Conscious Awareness III

This is a wonderful exercise for awareness.

Watch what is really being said and done around and within you. Now think of your Self inside, not the little you, but the big Self inside.

Totally surrender to Self. Constantly love it, and let it know you love it. Feel its constant warmth and flow.

Now watch and feel the scene of its possible conversation with you. Unbeknownst to you, you will be taken into this process of expanded awareness, and you will be able to tune into a new, greater consciousness.

As you practice this exercise over time, many of your dramas, traumas, anxieties, worries, and fears will fade away. Use your imagination in doing this exercise.

Try it now for just a few seconds. What was your experience? Reflect for a moment on it.

The more often you practice this exercise, the greater effect it will have in your life, which has previously been so full of reactions and disappointments. You will begin to feel relatively indifferent to the old dramas and situations to which you previously reacted.

Now with your heart and soul, feel the love coming into you. It is your new clothing. Consciously talk to it from inside your head—there's no need to talk out loud—and realize that it is a close friend.

In becoming aware, you will pick up more, you will realize more, and you will know more. That is what awareness is. You are taking it on; you are clothing yourself in it.

Think of your Self inside. Love it constantly, and let it know you love It. Feel its warmth and flow of it. It flows constantly, unending. As you watch what is really happening within and around you, you will observe a shift.

Grounding

Here is an exercise that is good for experiencing what healing energy feels like. You can do it anytime, anywhere. It happens to be helpful for those with moderate dyslexia, and it's good for calming an emotionally chaotic, confused, or over-stimulated state—what I sometimes call a bombarded mind.

The pads of our fingers act as terminals which both transmit and receive current. The first three fingers—the thumb, forefinger, and the middle finger—carry the greatest current. You can feel through the fingertips.

The left hand is a receiver. The right hand is a transmitter. When you gesture hello with the right hand, you are transmitting a blessing to that person.

Take your right hand and hold the first two fingers about one inch apart. Gently place them about one to one and a half inches above the eyebrows. You'll notice there are two slight indentations on your forehead, where they seem to naturally fit.

Barely touch your forehead with these fingers. If you leave your fingers there for a little while, you will begin to feel a slight sensation in your fingers and/or in your head, which will build up and then disperse. You may feel a building pressure. If that is the case, don't take your fingers away until you begin to feel the pressure disperse. You are dispersing chaotic energy. The effect will depend on your needs at that moment. Sometimes this process takes five seconds to complete, sometimes a little longer.

The Five-Finger Exercise

This simple exercise allows us to feel the energy, the Light, and the presence of the Divinity Within.

As you begin, your hands can be up or down—whatever is comfortable for you. Your hands and fingers will be barely touching. There is no need to rub your hands together to gather an electrical charge. Simply place the five fingers from each hand together in a kind of tent. Don't let your hands touch silk or wool, because that will create an unnecessary discharge and diminish the effect of the exercise. Don't press your fingers together; barely hold them there.

Then hold this position until you feel the full effect. You'll notice a feeling of heat or vibration between the palms, even if you have cold hands. Notice how it begins to build. It will increase. The palms will begin to tingle a little bit, and more life force will flow into the blood. Wait there until you feel the flow in your fingers or your hands. Actually, you are actually assisting the life force and its flow.

When you complete this exercise, it's counterproductive to shake your hand afterwards. Enjoy the aliveness of the energy.

Energy Stabilizing Exercise

To complete this exercise, you will need a partner. Stand up facing one another.

Take hold of the other person's hand.

Each of you is to cross your arms out in front of you so you are holding your partner's right hand with their left hand, and your left with their right hand.

Relax and close your eyes. Breathe in very slowly. Breathe in through your nose all the way down to your belly and gently and slowly out through your mouth. No heavy breathing. No hyperventilating. Slow and easy.

Imagine that you are feeling a sense of lightness filling your head. Become aware of your partner's size, shape, and temperature. Try to tune into that world, just for a moment.

Now begin to feel the energy flow between you as you are becoming more one with that person's energetics and less resistant to what that person might be thinking or feeling about you. Really get into it. Concentrate on the energy flow between each of you; imagine what it would be like to become one with the energy. The less resistance, the less the feelings of threat and fear, and the greater the flow. Let it flow. There is nothing to be afraid of once you begin to sense the energy.

Try to get in touch with the energy pull of that flow, of that energy called gravity. You will begin to sense the weight of its magnetism. It's a flow that is being established. Let it come into you. There's no need to resist or restrict it. Feel it flowing freely. Tap into and become aware of that flow a little bit more.

Open the bottoms of your feet as if they are vents and allow the earth's gravity to enter you. See it in your mind's eye, imagine it, feel it as a flow melting through you, slowly flowing up through your feet like thick orange lava, into your muscles, bones, and nerves. The vents in your feet will open up wider and wider.

Feel the weight of the energy, the raw power of it. Let it flow up through your ankles, your lower legs. It might feel uncomfortable at first; bear it; it's not going to hurt you. It will gently break through the areas of slowdown.

Feel the energy flow up from your knees, going up into your thighs, your hips, settling in your belly or lower back. Now feel it flow up through your chest and upper back and shoulders. It's a flow. It's magnetic. Let it flow through your arms and elbows. It will break through little areas of log-jams and then flow more freely.

Let the energy flow through your forearms, your wrists, your fingers, your hands. Let it break through. Nothing can stop it. Let your magnetic energy flow into your partner's fingers. Now that the flow is started, notice your breathing— how slow and soft it is.

Slowly open up your eyes. What was your experience?

Palm-to-Palm Exercise

This exercise also requires a partner. Make sure you are in a quiet environment so you can focus more easily.

Stand up and face your partner. Place your hands in the pat-a-cake position.

Bend your elbows at a ninety-degree angle, and turn your hands so one of your palms is facing the ceiling, the other facing the floor.

Put the left palm up and the right palm down. Have your partner do the same, so that your palms face each other's.

Your palms should not be touching. Hold your palms one to one and a half inches away from your partner. Do not make physical contact.

Close your eyes. Begin to feel the energy between your hands. Feel it on your palms. That energy within you is waiting and begging for you to give it. It is the life force that is flowing between you. That's the flow of energy. Slowly start to move your hand up and down a little bit, maybe an inch or two. Feel this on the skin of your hands. Move slowly.

Continue to move your hands slowly up and down a little. Feel the attraction and the pull of the energy. It will feel like a pressure inside. You will feel something between your hands. Experience the inner and outer limits of the electrical matrix of the body. Feel how alive it is. How tall it is. How wide around the hand it is. It will vary with everyone you practice with and has nothing to do with your control. Move your hands apart until you barely feel the energy, and open your eyes to see how far apart your hands are.

You are feeling the electromagnetic bond that we are all composed of; it is the extrusion of the spiritual body.

If while you are doing this, you feel something in a particular part of your body, that is because you breaking up a logjam of pent-up energy. If, say, you feel something in your wrist, maybe that energy was a wrist injury or even carpal tunnel syndrome. The flow of energy is clearing the logjam in that spot.

Glossary

Alchemical. I use this term as referring to a subtle or substantial internal integration of changes in the thinking, emotions, and body. This takes place through an internal blending of earth and heaven, making the individual more whole. The outcome is to purify and integrate change. Alchemy also has to do with the transmutation of mind and matter.

Auras. Intangible emanations, perceived as colors, light, sound, odor, or visions from a person or object, transmitting information about that person or object's past, present, and potential experiences. See also **morphic fields**.

Causal moment. An introduction to future events. Any event or series of events that leads to another event. The original understanding of a synchronistic event. In healing, causal moments are primarily seen as past dramas and traumas embedded in our self-conversations, which keep us tied to a sense of lack and limitation. The term also relates to spiritual events that might have produced a shock or trauma within the mind, emotions, or body. Causal moments most often result from a willing disconnection from Source. A causal moment is also seen as a current moment of choice that can determine future effects. It's never the end of the story.

Concentrated focus. A purposeful state of intense attention that knows and perceives beyond normal appearances; a sustained holding of the image in perfection.

Conscious awareness. Becoming more aware and attentive to what is going on internally and externally within and around you in the linear or nonlinear world.

Directed meditation and exercises. Guided exercises that lead to a specific internal experience or answer, either in a personal or communal setting. They can lead to events of awareness in the mind of the Creator, God, or Self.

Disease, or dis-ease. A state of discomfort or ill health in body or mind, manifesting as a result of past dramas and traumas caused by an internalized perceptual event.

Downtime. A time of slowing down and regrouping, brought about either consciously or subconsciously. Downtimes are often generated as aftereffects from an intense time of creativity or a destructive event. After a flow of uplifting events, we tend to crash into disarray or depression. Usually these times are made for us to integrate what we have just gone through.

Dramas and traumas. Self-inflicted conversations that sabotage and derail us from clear, objective thinking, usually originating from negative perceptions of judgment, blame, guilt, and other influences of mass mind. Dramas and traumas tend to originate in causal moments that we have interpreted as loss, hurt, danger, or anger. At these times, we tend to negate or ignore the Self and its guidance and direction.

Free choice. The use of free will to act, to hear the voice of Self (God, Creator, or the Divine Within) through our intuitive abilities and to accept its guidance and direction. The ability to remove ourselves from the influence of dramas and traumas.

Genetic code. The collective memory of our every experience within the soul, handed down into the genes to influence and be carried by the flow of the neural receptors within the body. The genetic code can be observed consciously as we learn stillness without resistance.

God. Also called Creator, Self, Nameless One, Divinity Within, and by many other names. Living consciousness; the Source of love, life, guidance, and direction.

Human-in-being. The state of being actualized, of experiencing one's Self and its forgiveness. Going beyond the limitations of mass mind to know our true nature and living in its mind. Living in actualized wisdom. Experiencing compassion more fully.

Imagination. "Imaging-in-action": the process of understanding or picturing something as already existing, either in its destructive form or in its perfect, creative form. Imagination is based upon our memory of experiences.

Inner teaching or inner voice. The still, small voice within. The guidance and direction given to us by our Divinity Within and through Self. The sharing from our Source within as an image, a knowing revealed to us of something that is in the process of manifestation. The voice of Self gives us guidance and direction, often interpreted as an idea, thought, or revelation from within.

Law of cause and effect. States that for every action, there is an equal and opposite reaction, both in the linear world and in the nonlinear world of synchronicity. The universal principle that every cause has an effect and every effect has another cause, which is the basis for understanding causal moments. Each effect is a reciprocation for a previous word, thought, and action.

Magnetic energy. A part of the electromagnetic matrix that holds together each thing in a specific pattern, form, and shape; also referred to as electromagnetic energy. In our universe, electrical and magnetic energy cannot exist without the other; they are intermeshed.

Mantra. A word or phrase repeated in meditation, to focus the person on a particular aspect of God in their life. The mantra is used to bring us closer to our Source.

Mass mind. The influences that we learn and carry within us deriving from families, friends, and what we witness and experience. Cultural influences based upon either constructive self-acceptance from the intuitive guidance from the Self or destructive fear and separation.

Meditation. A state of focused communion and communication. A sense of union, utilizing the quiet mind to experience oneness within the mind of God, Creator, Universal Consciousness. Meditation enables us to ask a question and receive an answer according to our needs and growth.

Morphic fields. Nonlinear emanations of information within and around our being, derived from past, present, and potentially future events. Also referred to as **auras.**

Nameless One. An ancient name for Creator, the Divine Being, God, Self, or Universal Mind.

Prayer. The manifestation of everything that emanates from within us to create patterns within ourselves and in the world; the manifestation of what we choose for ourselves. What is in the heart comes out of the mouth in our actions and thoughts. Every word, thought, and action is a living prayer. Prayer can be used to obtain things or growth for ourselves and others. Prayer can also be for thanks and adoration to our Source. It is our moment to capture the attention of God.

Reincarnation. Living over many lifetimes; the activity and the experience of our soul since the beginnings of time. Reincarnation accounts for all that has made us who we are, what we are, and why we are, through the evolutionary process of getting to know our Self.

Revelation. The stimulation of understanding of the Self within as it speaks through purity from the mind of the Creator.

Sabotage. An action that discounts our own experience of Self; the process of blocking, limiting, or undermining the guidance and insights we receive from within.

Scanning. A tool utilized as part of the healing process. The ability to go within to one's own or another's morphic fields through intuitive sight to work with disturbances and distortions. Scanning is often used to determine previous causal events of drama and trauma.

Self. The living expression of the Divine Within. That which is our life.

Synchronicity. The continuum of cause and effect, linking everything together in harmonious flow, without beginning or end. A ripple effect that leads to new effects ad infinitum.

Printed in the USA
CPSIA information can be obtained
at www.ICGtesting.com
JSHW011358061123
51534JS00013B/120